Iowa
Assessments
Success Strategies
Level 12 Grade 6

DEAR FUTURE EXAM SUCCESS STORY

First of all, **THANK YOU** for purchasing Mometrix study materials!

Second, congratulations! You are one of the few determined test-takers who are committed to doing whatever it takes to excel on your exam. **You have come to the right place.** We developed these study materials with one goal in mind: to deliver you the information you need in a format that's concise and easy to use.

In addition to optimizing your guide for the content of the test, we've outlined our recommended steps for breaking down the preparation process into small, attainable goals so you can make sure you stay on track.

We've also analyzed the entire test-taking process, identifying the most common pitfalls and showing how you can overcome them and be ready for any curveball the test throws you.

Standardized testing is one of the biggest obstacles on your road to success, which only increases the importance of doing well in the high-pressure, high-stakes environment of test day. Your results on this test could have a significant impact on your future, and this guide provides the information and practical advice to help you achieve your full potential on test day.

Your success is our success

We would love to hear from you! If you would like to share the story of your exam success or if you have any questions or comments in regard to our products, please contact us at **800-673-8175** or **support@mometrix.com**.

Thanks again for your business and we wish you continued success!

Sincerely,
The Mometrix Test Preparation Team

TABLE OF CONTENTS

Introduction

Thank you for purchasing this resource! You have made the choice to prepare yourself for a test that could have a huge impact on your future, and this guide is designed to help you be fully ready for test day. Obviously, it's important to have a solid understanding of the test material, but you also need to be prepared for the unique environment and stressors of the test, so that you can perform to the best of your abilities.

For this purpose, the first section that appears in this guide is the **Success Strategies**. We've devoted countless hours to meticulously researching what works and what doesn't, and we've boiled down our findings to the five most impactful steps you can take to improve your performance on the test. We start at the beginning with study planning and move through the preparation process, all the way to the testing strategies that will help you get the most out of what you know when you're finally sitting in front of the test.

We recommend that you start preparing for your test as far in advance as possible. However, if you've bought this guide as a last-minute study resource and only have a few days before your test, we recommend that you skip over the first two Success Strategies since they address a long-term study plan.

If you struggle with **test anxiety**, we strongly encourage you to check out our recommendations for how you can overcome it. Test anxiety is a formidable foe, but it can be beaten, and we want to make sure you have the tools you need to defeat it.

Strategy #1 – Plan Big, Study Small

There's a lot riding on your performance. If you want to ace this test, you're going to need to keep your skills sharp and the material fresh in your mind. You need a plan that lets you review everything you need to know while still fitting in your schedule. We'll break this strategy down into three categories.

Information Organization

Start with the information you already have: the official test outline. From this, you can make a complete list of all the concepts you need to cover before the test. Organize these concepts into groups that can be studied together, and create a list of any related vocabulary you need to learn so you can brush up on any difficult terms. You'll want to keep this vocabulary list handy once you actually start studying since you may need to add to it along the way.

Time Management

Once you have your set of study concepts, decide how to spread them out over the time you have left before the test. Break your study plan into small, clear goals so you have a manageable task for each day and know exactly what you're doing. Then just focus on one small step at a time. When you manage your time this way, you don't need to spend hours at a time studying. Studying a small block of content for a short period each day helps you retain information better and avoid stressing over how much you have left to do. You can relax knowing that you have a plan to cover everything in time. In order for this strategy to be effective though, you have to start studying early and stick to your schedule. Avoid the exhaustion and futility that comes from last-minute cramming!

Study Environment

The environment you study in has a big impact on your learning. Studying in a coffee shop, while probably more enjoyable, is not likely to be as fruitful as studying in a quiet room. It's important to keep distractions to a minimum. You're only planning to study for a short block of time, so make the most of it. Don't pause to check your phone or get up to find a snack. It's also important to **avoid multitasking**. Research has consistently shown that multitasking will make your studying dramatically less effective. Your study area should also be comfortable and well-lit so you don't have the distraction of straining your eyes or sitting on an uncomfortable chair.

 The time of day you study is also important. You want to be rested and alert. Don't wait until just before bedtime. Study when you'll be most likely to comprehend and remember. Even better, if you know what time of day your test will be, set that time aside for study. That way your brain will be used to working on that subject at that specific time and you'll have a better chance of recalling information.

Finally, it can be helpful to team up with others who are studying for the same test. Your actual studying should be done in as isolated an environment as possible, but the work of organizing the information and setting up the study plan can be divided up. In between study sessions, you can discuss with your teammates the concepts that you're all studying and quiz each other on the details. Just be sure that your teammates are as serious about the test as you are. If you find that your study time is being replaced with social time, you might need to find a new team.

Strategy #2 – Make Your Studying Count

You're devoting a lot of time and effort to preparing for this test, so you want to be absolutely certain it will pay off. This means doing more than just reading the content and hoping you can remember it on test day. It's important to make every minute of study count. There are two main areas you can focus on to make your studying count.

Retention

It doesn't matter how much time you study if you can't remember the material. You need to make sure you are retaining the concepts. To check your retention of the information you're learning, try recalling it at later times with minimal prompting. Try carrying around flashcards and glance at one or two from time to time or ask a friend who's also studying for the test to quiz you.

To enhance your retention, look for ways to put the information into practice so that you can apply it rather than simply recalling it. If you're using the information in practical ways, it will be much easier to remember. Similarly, it helps to solidify a concept in your mind if you're not only reading it to yourself but also explaining it to someone else. Ask a friend to let you teach them about a concept you're a little shaky on (or speak aloud to an imaginary audience if necessary). As you try to summarize, define, give examples, and answer your friend's questions, you'll understand the concepts better and they will stay with you longer. Finally, step back for a big picture view and ask yourself how each piece of information fits with the whole subject. When you link the different concepts together and see them working together as a whole, it's easier to remember the individual components.

Finally, practice showing your work on any multi-step problems, even if you're just studying. Writing out each step you take to solve a problem will help solidify the process in your mind, and you'll be more likely to remember it during the test.

Modality

Modality simply refers to the means or method by which you study. Choosing a study modality that fits your own individual learning style is crucial. No two people learn best in exactly the same way, so it's important to know your strengths and use them to your advantage.

For example, if you learn best by visualization, focus on visualizing a concept in your mind and draw an image or a diagram. Try color-coding your notes, illustrating them, or creating symbols that will trigger your mind to recall a learned concept. If you learn best by hearing or discussing information, find a study partner who learns the same way or read aloud to yourself. Think about how to put the information in your own words. Imagine that you are giving a lecture on the topic and record yourself so you can listen to it later.

For any learning style, flashcards can be helpful. Organize the information so you can take advantage of spare moments to review. Underline key words or phrases. Use different colors for different categories. Mnemonic devices (such as creating a short list in which every item starts with the same letter) can also help with retention. Find what works best for you and use it to store the information in your mind most effectively and easily.

3

Strategy #3 – Practice the Right Way

Your success on test day depends not only on how many hours you put into preparing, but also on whether you prepared the right way. It's good to check along the way to see if your studying is paying off. One of the most effective ways to do this is by taking practice tests to evaluate your progress. Practice tests are useful because they show exactly where you need to improve. Every time you take a practice test, pay special attention to these three groups of questions:

- The questions you got wrong
- The questions you had to guess on, even if you guessed right
- The questions you found difficult or slow to work through

This will show you exactly what your weak areas are, and where you need to devote more study time. Ask yourself why each of these questions gave you trouble. Was it because you didn't understand the material? Was it because you didn't remember the vocabulary? Do you need more repetitions on this type of question to build speed and confidence? Dig into those questions and figure out how you can strengthen your weak areas as you go back to review the material.

 Additionally, many practice tests have a section explaining the answer choices. It can be tempting to read the explanation and think that you now have a good understanding of the concept. However, an explanation likely only covers part of the question's broader context. Even if the explanation makes perfect sense, **go back and investigate** every concept related to the question until you're positive you have a thorough understanding.

As you go along, keep in mind that the practice test is just that: practice. Memorizing these questions and answers will not be very helpful on the actual test because it is unlikely to have any of the same exact questions. If you only know the right answers to the sample questions, you won't be prepared for the real thing. **Study the concepts** until you understand them fully, and then you'll be able to answer any question that shows up on the test.

It's important to wait on the practice tests until you're ready. If you take a test on your first day of study, you may be overwhelmed by the amount of material covered and how much you need to learn. Work up to it gradually.

On test day, you'll need to be prepared for answering questions, managing your time, and using the test-taking strategies you've learned. It's a lot to balance, like a mental marathon that will have a big impact on your future. Like training for a marathon, you'll need to start slowly and work your way up. When test day arrives, you'll be ready.

Start with the strategies you've read in the first two Success Strategies—plan your course and study in the way that works best for you. If you have time, consider using multiple study resources to get different approaches to the same concepts. It can be helpful to see difficult concepts from more than one angle. Then find a good source for practice tests. Many times, the test website will suggest potential study resources or provide sample tests.

4

Practice Test Strategy

If you're able to find at least three practice tests, we recommend this strategy:

UNTIMED AND OPEN-BOOK PRACTICE

Take the first test with no time constraints and with your notes and study guide handy. Take your time and focus on applying the strategies you've learned.

TIMED AND OPEN-BOOK PRACTICE

Take the second practice test open-book as well, but set a timer and practice pacing yourself to finish in time.

TIMED AND CLOSED-BOOK PRACTICE

Take any other practice tests as if it were test day. Set a timer and put away your study materials. Sit at a table or desk in a quiet room, imagine yourself at the testing center, and answer questions as quickly and accurately as possible.

Keep repeating timed and closed-book tests on a regular basis until you run out of practice tests or it's time for the actual test. Your mind will be ready for the schedule and stress of test day, and you'll be able to focus on recalling the material you've learned.

Strategy #4 – Pace Yourself

Once you're fully prepared for the material on the test, your biggest challenge on test day will be managing your time. Just knowing that the clock is ticking can make you panic even if you have plenty of time left. Work on pacing yourself so you can build confidence against the time constraints of the exam. Pacing is a difficult skill to master, especially in a high-pressure environment, so **practice is vital**.

Set time expectations for your pace based on how much time is available. For example, if a section has 60 questions and the time limit is 30 minutes, you know you have to average 30 seconds or less per question in order to answer them all. Although 30 seconds is the hard limit, set 25 seconds per question as your goal, so you reserve extra time to spend on harder questions. When you budget extra time for the harder questions, you no longer have any reason to stress when those questions take longer to answer.

Don't let this time expectation distract you from working through the test at a calm, steady pace, but keep it in mind so you don't spend too much time on any one question. Recognize that taking extra time on one question you don't understand may keep you from answering two that you do understand later in the test. If your time limit for a question is up and you're still not sure of the answer, mark it and move on, and come back to it later if the time and the test format allow. If the testing format doesn't allow you to return to earlier questions, just make an educated guess; then put it out of your mind and move on.

On the easier questions, be careful not to rush. It may seem wise to hurry through them so you have more time for the challenging ones, but it's not worth missing one if you know the concept and just didn't take the time to read the question fully. Work efficiently but make sure you understand the question and have looked at all of the answer choices, since more than one may seem right at first.

Even if you're paying attention to the time, you may find yourself a little behind at some point. You should speed up to get back on track, but do so wisely. Don't panic; just take a few seconds less on each question until you're caught up. Don't guess without thinking, but do look through the answer choices and eliminate any you know are wrong. If you can get down to two choices, it is often worthwhile to guess from those. Once you've chosen an answer, move on and don't dwell on any that you skipped or had to hurry through. If a question was taking too long, chances are it was one of the harder ones, so you weren't as likely to get it right anyway.

On the other hand, if you find yourself getting ahead of schedule, it may be beneficial to slow down a little. The more quickly you work, the more likely you are to make a careless mistake that will affect your score. You've budgeted time for each question, so don't be afraid to spend that time. Practice an efficient but careful pace to get the most out of the time you have.

Test-Taking Strategies

This section contains a list of test-taking strategies that you may find helpful as you work through the test. By taking what you know and applying logical thought, you can maximize your chances of answering any question correctly!

It is very important to realize that every question is different and every person is different: no single strategy will work on every question, and no single strategy will work for every person. That's why we've included all of them here, so you can try them out and determine which ones work best for different types of questions and which ones work best for you.

Question Strategies

⊘ READ CAREFULLY

Read the question and the answer choices carefully. Don't miss the question because you misread the terms. You have plenty of time to read each question thoroughly and make sure you understand what is being asked. Yet a happy medium must be attained, so don't waste too much time. You must read carefully and efficiently.

⊘ CONTEXTUAL CLUES

Look for contextual clues. If the question includes a word you are not familiar with, look at the immediate context for some indication of what the word might mean. Contextual clues can often give you all the information you need to decipher the meaning of an unfamiliar word. Even if you can't determine the meaning, you may be able to narrow down the possibilities enough to make a solid guess at the answer to the question.

⊘ PREFIXES

If you're having trouble with a word in the question or answer choices, try dissecting it. Take advantage of every clue that the word might include. Prefixes can be a huge help. Usually, they allow you to determine a basic meaning. *Pre-* means before, *post-* means after, *pro-* is positive, *de-* is negative. From prefixes, you can get an idea of the general meaning of the word and try to put it into context.

⊘ HEDGE WORDS

Watch out for critical hedge words, such as *likely, may, can, sometimes, often, almost, mostly, usually, generally, rarely,* and *sometimes.* Question writers insert these hedge phrases to cover every possibility. Often an answer choice will be wrong simply because it leaves no room for exception. Be on guard for answer choices that have definitive words such as *exactly* and *always.*

⊘ SWITCHBACK WORDS

Stay alert for *switchbacks*. These are the words and phrases frequently used to alert you to shifts in thought. The most common switchback words are *but, although,* and *however*. Others include *nevertheless, on the other hand, even though, while, in spite of, despite,* and *regardless of.* Switchback words are important to catch because they can change the direction of the question or an answer choice.

7

⊘ Face Value

When in doubt, use common sense. Accept the situation in the problem at face value. Don't read too much into it. These problems will not require you to make wild assumptions. If you have to go beyond creativity and warp time or space in order to have an answer choice fit the question, then you should move on and consider the other answer choices. These are normal problems rooted in reality. The applicable relationship or explanation may not be readily apparent, but it is there for you to figure out. Use your common sense to interpret anything that isn't clear.

Answer Choice Strategies

⊘ Answer Selection

The most thorough way to pick an answer choice is to identify and eliminate wrong answers until only one is left, then confirm it is the correct answer. Sometimes an answer choice may immediately seem right, but be careful. The test writers will usually put more than one reasonable answer choice on each question, so take a second to read all of them and make sure that the other choices are not equally obvious. As long as you have time left, it is better to read every answer choice than to pick the first one that looks right without checking the others.

⊘ Answer Choice Families

An answer choice family consists of two (in rare cases, three) answer choices that are very similar in construction and cannot all be true at the same time. If you see two answer choices that are direct opposites or parallels, one of them is usually the correct answer. For instance, if one answer choice says that quantity x increases and another either says that quantity x decreases (opposite) or says that quantity y increases (parallel), then those answer choices would fall into the same family. An answer choice that doesn't match the construction of the answer choice family is more likely to be incorrect. Most questions will not have answer choice families, but when they do appear, you should be prepared to recognize them.

⊘ Eliminate Answers

Eliminate answer choices as soon as you realize they are wrong, but make sure you consider all possibilities. If you are eliminating answer choices and realize that the last one you are left with is also wrong, don't panic. Start over and consider each choice again. There may be something you missed the first time that you will realize on the second pass.

⊘ Avoid Fact Traps

Don't be distracted by an answer choice that is factually true but doesn't answer the question. You are looking for the choice that answers the question. Stay focused on what the question is asking for so you don't accidentally pick an answer that is true but incorrect. Always go back to the question and make sure the answer choice you've selected actually answers the question and is not merely a true statement.

⊘ Extreme Statements

In general, you should avoid answers that put forth extreme actions as standard practice or proclaim controversial ideas as established fact. An answer choice that states the "process should be used in certain situations, if..." is much more likely to be correct than one that states the "process should be discontinued completely." The first is a calm rational statement and doesn't even make a definitive, uncompromising stance, using a hedge word *if* to provide wiggle room, whereas the second choice is far more extreme.

⊘ BENCHMARK

As you read through the answer choices and you come across one that seems to answer the question well, mentally select that answer choice. This is not your final answer, but it's the one that will help you evaluate the other answer choices. The one that you selected is your benchmark or standard for judging each of the other answer choices. Every other answer choice must be compared to your benchmark. That choice is correct until proven otherwise by another answer choice beating it. If you find a better answer, then that one becomes your new benchmark. Once you've decided that no other choice answers the question as well as your benchmark, you have your final answer.

⊘ PREDICT THE ANSWER

Before you even start looking at the answer choices, it is often best to try to predict the answer. When you come up with the answer on your own, it is easier to avoid distractions and traps because you will know exactly what to look for. The right answer choice is unlikely to be word-for-word what you came up with, but it should be a close match. Even if you are confident that you have the right answer, you should still take the time to read each option before moving on.

General Strategies

⊘ TOUGH QUESTIONS

If you are stumped on a problem or it appears too hard or too difficult, don't waste time. Move on! Remember though, if you can quickly check for obviously incorrect answer choices, your chances of guessing correctly are greatly improved. Before you completely give up, at least try to knock out a couple of possible answers. Eliminate what you can and then guess at the remaining answer choices before moving on.

⊘ CHECK YOUR WORK

Since you will probably not know every term listed and the answer to every question, it is important that you get credit for the ones that you do know. Don't miss any questions through careless mistakes. If at all possible, try to take a second to look back over your answer selection and make sure you've selected the correct answer choice and haven't made a costly careless mistake (such as marking an answer choice that you didn't mean to mark). This quick double check should more than pay for itself in caught mistakes for the time it costs.

⊘ PACE YOURSELF

It's easy to be overwhelmed when you're looking at a page full of questions; your mind is confused and full of random thoughts, and the clock is ticking down faster than you would like. Calm down and maintain the pace that you have set for yourself. Especially as you get down to the last few minutes of the test, don't let the small numbers on the clock make you panic. As long as you are on track by monitoring your pace, you are guaranteed to have time for each question.

⊘ DON'T RUSH

It is very easy to make errors when you are in a hurry. Maintaining a fast pace in answering questions is pointless if it makes you miss questions that you would have gotten right otherwise. Test writers like to include distracting information and wrong answers that seem right. Taking a little extra time to avoid careless mistakes can make all the difference in your test score. Find a pace that allows you to be confident in the answers that you select.

⊘ Keep Moving

Panicking will not help you pass the test, so do your best to stay calm and keep moving. Taking deep breaths and going through the answer elimination steps you practiced can help to break through a stress barrier and keep your pace.

Final Notes

The combination of a solid foundation of content knowledge and the confidence that comes from practicing your plan for applying that knowledge is the key to maximizing your performance on test day. As your foundation of content knowledge is built up and strengthened, you'll find that the strategies included in this chapter become more and more effective in helping you quickly sift through the distractions and traps of the test to isolate the correct answer.

Now that you're preparing to move forward into the test content chapters of this book, be sure to keep your goal in mind. As you read, think about how you will be able to apply this information on the test. If you've already seen sample questions for the test and you have an idea of the question format and style, try to come up with questions of your own that you can answer based on what you're reading. This will give you valuable practice applying your knowledge in the same ways you can expect to on test day.

Good luck and good studying!

Practice Test

Reading

Reading is one of the keys to success in school and in life. Being able to read well opens the door to all sorts of opportunities and adventures, in many different areas. That's why reading is emphasized so much in school. Being a good reader is vital to doing well in school, at college, and in a career. No matter what level of reading skills you possess right now, you can improve upon them. There are no secrets or mysteries when it comes to reading skills; you simply need to work to make improvements. You have what it takes to be a good reader, and these exercises will help you as you strive to raise your reading skills.

Questions 1 – 12 pertain to the following short story:

A WORLD OF WHITE: THE IDITAROD TRAIL

(1) Imagine clinging desperately to your sled as brutal winds batter your body. The path ahead appears and disappears like a mirage, frequently obscured by blowing curtains of snow. You are freezing and sweating at the same time. Your throat burns with thirst, and your body aches with fatigue. You know your dogs must feel it too, so you encourage them to press on to the next checkpoint. All around you, the world is endless, empty, and white. Welcome to the Iditarod Trail.

(2) Alaska's Iditarod Trail is the world's most famous sled dog racing venue. But the trail is older than the sport of sled dog racing. In fact, the Iditarod Trail was first established in the early 1900s, during the Alaskan gold rush. In those days, dog teams were used for work, hauling thousands of pounds of gold from landlocked Iditarod to the port of Anchorage. But in faraway Nome, also known for gold, six-year-old George Allen had the idea to put together a race to see whose sled dogs were fastest, and the sport of sled dog racing was born.

(3) Though the Iditarod Trail race is the most famous race in the sport of sled dog racing, the first race along the trail was actually a race to save lives. In 1925, a diphtheria outbreak began in Nome. To prevent an epidemic that could kill thousands, doctors were desperate for the vaccine serum, but the closest serum was in Anchorage. The train ran from Anchorage to the village of Nenana, but that was still 674 miles from Nome. A cry for help was sent by the doctors, and in the midst of the blizzards and windstorms of January, the call was answered. Twenty brave mushers drove their dogs in a frantic relay, carrying 300,000 bottles of serum from Nenana to Nome. They followed the Iditarod Trail.

(4) Dog sledding, or "mushing," became quite popular after that heroic journey, but by the 1960s, it had lost popularity and the Iditarod Trail had been largely forgotten. There were a few lovers of mushing, however, who worked tirelessly to reestablish the Iditarod Trail and create a new sled dog race that used the trail as its course. The first official race was held in 1967 to celebrate the centennial of the purchase of Alaska from Russia. The race involved 58 drivers who mushed 56 miles in two days. This race was a success, but the popularity and future of the Iditarod Trail was still in question.

(5) In March of 1973, the first Anchorage to Nome Iditarod Trail race was organized and held. This race was much longer than previous races, covering more than 1,000 miles—the whole Iditarod Trail. Thirty-four mushers began the race, but only 22 were able to finish. After the 1973 race, the popularity of the Iditarod Trail finally grew and was firmly established. In 1978, the Iditarod Trail became a National Historic Trail.

(6) The modern Iditarod Trail race is open to mushers over 18 years old who have qualified in a recognized race of 200 miles or more. For younger mushers between 14 and 18 years old, the Junior Iditarod offers a 130-mile version of the race. Many Junior Iditarod participants go on to compete in the Iditarod Trail race, as the Junior Iditarod is good practice for the grueling trek of the main race. All mushers must prepare for the race extensively, often for months before the race. Many mushers run their dogs more than 1,500 miles in preparation, giving them experience in all types of weather and terrain.

(7) To enter the Iditarod Trail race, participants must pay an entrance fee. Then they must travel to Anchorage with their dogs. In Anchorage, they attend a mushers' banquet where they are given their racing order numbers. Afterwards, all participating dogs are checked by a veterinarian and marked by race officials to prevent dog switching mid-race, which is not allowed. The dogs are even drug tested at the beginning and at checkpoints throughout the race to prevent cheating! Finally, the sleds and equipment are checked. Then participants are ready to start the race.

(8) On the morning of the Iditarod Trail race, mushers leave Anchorage in their assigned racing order. They are sent out one at a time, at two-minute intervals. For more than a week—sometimes up to three weeks—they travel throughout Alaska, stopping at designated checkpoints all along the Iditarod Trail as they make their way to Nome. When all participants have reached Nome, another mushers' banquet is held. Awards are given, and everyone is applauded for their achievement. Win or lose, the mushers know that only the toughest of the tough have what it takes to finish the race and conquer the great Iditarod Trail.

1. What does the simile in paragraph 1 describe?

    a. The snow
    b. The path
    c. The musher's throat
    d. The dogs

2. What does "landlocked" mean in paragraph 2?

    a. Barricaded by hills
    b. Built underground
    c. Not on a waterway
    d. In the mountains

3. What two cities are on the ends of the Iditarod Trail?

    a. Anchorage and Nome
    b. Nome and Nenana
    c. Iditarod and Anchorage
    d. Nenana and Iditarod

4. What is the author's main purpose in writing this article?

    a. To encourage mushers to race on the Iditarod Trail

    b. To inform the reader about the 1925 diphtheria outbreak

    c. To describe the terrain of Alaska

    d. To educate the reader about the Iditarod Trail

5. In paragraph 3, which words best convey the feelings of the doctors in Nome in 1925?

    a. "Epidemic" and "diphtheria"

    b. "Blizzards" and "windstorms"

    c. "Brave" and "frantic relay"

    d. "Desperate" and "cry for help"

6. Why did the author choose to write this article in third-person point of view?

    a. Historical overviews are best written in third person

    b. The author has never been to Alaska

    c. Third person is the required point of view in nonfiction writing

    d. This article is not written in third-person point of view

7. In what year did the Iditarod Trail become a National Historic Trail?

    a. 1967

    b. 1973

    c. 1978

    d. 1981

8. Which of the following is the best summary of the history of the Iditarod Trail race?

    a. After the Iditarod Trail became a National Historic Trail, the race became more popular, and today many mushers participate each year

    b. After a slow start in 1967, the Iditarod Trail race became firmly established in 1973, and it continues in popularity today

    c. In the first race in 1973, 34 mushers began the race, but only 22 were able to finish, proving that the race was just too hard

    d. Mushers between 14 and 18 years of age can race in the Junior Iditarod, while those over 18 can participate in the main race if they qualify

9. How is this article organized?

    a. Chronologically

    b. Geographically

    c. Randomly

    d. Spatially

10. Which of the following is a supporting detail in this article?

    a. Alaska's Iditarod Trail is the world's most famous sled dog racing venue

    b. After the heroic journey of 1925, mushing became more popular

    c. Some mushers run their dogs over 1,500 miles to prepare for the race

    d. There are specific requirements to enter the Iditarod Trail race

11. What do participants receive at the first mushers' banquet?

    a. Awards
    b. Racing order numbers
    c. Supplies
    d. Trail maps

12. What is the interval used to separate mushers as they begin the Iditarod Trail race?

    a. Five minutes
    b. One minute
    c. Ten minutes
    d. Two minutes

Questions 13 –24 pertain to the following story:

THE RIGHT THING TO DO

Characters *(in order of appearance)*:

JESSICA—a sixth-grade girl, Amy's friend

GROUP OF FRIENDS—a group of sixth-grade girls

AMY—a sixth-grade girl, Jessica's friend

SALES CLERK—a clerk in the store Amy and Jessica visit

Scene 1

(1) *Jessica stands with a group of friends on the school steps. The group is chatting and laughing. Amy approaches from stage right.*

(2) AMY: Jessica! Jessica!

(3) JESSICA: *(turning away from her friends and taking a step toward Amy)* Hi, Amy. What's up?

(4) AMY: I'm headed to the mall, and I thought you might want to come.

(5) JESSICA: Why me? I thought we weren't friends anymore.

(6) AMY: *(waving her hand and shaking her head)* That old fight? Ancient history. So … do you want to come or not?

(7) JESSICA: *(glancing back at her friends)* Sure. I'll come. Just give me a minute.

(8) *Jessica runs back and talks with her friends for a moment, then rejoins Amy. Amy and Jessica exit stage right.*

Scene 2

(9) *Amy and Jessica are looking at a shelf full of lipstick in a cosmetics store in the mall.*

(10) AMY: Look at this one, Jess. Don't you just love this color? *(She picks up a lipstick tube.)*

(11) JESSICA: It's nice, but I like this one better. *(She picks up a different tube of lipstick.)*

(12) *A sales clerk enters from stage left.*

(13) SALES CLERK: *(stopping by the girls)* Can I help you ladies find something?

(14) AMY: Oh, no. We're just looking.

(15) JESSICA: Thank you, though.

(16) SALES CLERK: Okay. Well, let me know if you need anything. *(He/she exits stage right.)*

(17) AMY: So, which one are you going to get?

(18) JESSICA: *(looking at the floor and shaking her head)* I'm not getting one. They're a little spendy for me. Besides, I'm saving up for something special.

(19) AMY: *(laughing)* Who said anything about money? *(She slips her favorite lipstick into her pocket.)* I didn't ask you which one you were going to buy. I asked which one you were going to get. So, which one will it be?

(20) JESSICA: But—but—that's stealing!

(21) AMY: Look at all these tubes of lipstick. They'll never miss a couple.

(22) JESSICA: *(looking around nervously)* What if that sales clerk comes back and catches us?

(23) AMY: You worry too much. *(She picks up two tubes of lipstick.)* Now, was this the one you liked? Or was it this one? Never mind. We'll take them both. *(She slips them both into her pocket.)*

(24) JESSICA: Amy! This is wrong. We shouldn't be doing this.

(25) AMY: *(glaring at Jessica)* Do you even want to be my friend again? It sure doesn't sound like it.

(26) JESSICA: Of course I want to be your friend. It's just—

(27) AMY: Then come on. Let's go. *(She starts to walk away, and then turns and looks back.)* Are you coming?

(28) JESSICA: Fine. *(She follows Amy.)* But what if the alarm goes off?

(29) AMY: For a couple of tubes of lipstick? Not gonna happen. Now, follow me. And for heaven's sake, don't look so nervous.

(30) *The girls exit stage right.*

Scene 3

(31) *Jessica reenters the cosmetics store from stage right. She stops at the shelf of lipsticks and looks around. The sales clerk enters from stage left.*

(32) JESSICA: Excuse me ...

(33) SALES CLERK: *(stopping)* Did you need help with something?

(34) JESSICA: Yes. *(She looks at the floor.)* My friend who was just with me, um, she took—well, actually, she stole three tubes of lipstick. I'm not okay with that. So, um, I wanted to pay for them.

(35) SALES CLERK: That's impressive. I've never seen that happen before. And kids take stuff from this store all the time. What made you come back?

(36) JESSICA: *(shrugging)* I don't know. I guess it was just the right thing to do.

13. In paragraph 6, what does Amy mean when she calls her fight with Jessica "ancient history"?
   a. It happened thousands of years ago
   b. It happened in history class
   c. Amy has totally forgotten about the fight
   d. They were arguing about events in ancient history

14. What is the setting for Scene 1?
   a. The school steps
   b. The mall
   c. A cosmetics store
   d. Amy's house

15. What is the setting for Scene 2 and Scene 3?
   a. The school steps
   b. Jessica's house
   c. A cosmetics store
   d. Amy's house

16. Which scene contains the climax of this play?
   a. Scene 1
   b. Scene 2
   c. Scene 3
   d. All of the above

17. Which scene contains the denouement of this play?
   a. Scene 1
   b. Scene 2
   c. Scene 3
   d. All of the above

18. In paragraph 29, why is the word "gonna" considered acceptable?

a. It shows Amy's pattern of slang speech
b. It is always acceptable in written English
c. It is a different language spoken by Amy
d. It is not acceptable; it is a misspelling

19. In paragraph 6, what type of figurative language is used when Amy says "ancient history"?

a. Metaphor
b. Simile
c. Personification
d. Hyperbole

20. Which of the following best describes the overall tone of this play?

a. Formal
b. Conversational
c. Classical
d. Musical

21. What is the underlying theme of this play?

a. Amy and Jessica are best friends
b. Doing the right thing is always a good decision
c. It is okay to steal if you are not caught
d. Shopping for cosmetics increases peer pressure

22. Which paragraph best shows Amy's justification for stealing the lipstick?

a. Paragraph 21
b. Paragraph 23
c. Paragraph 25
d. Paragraph 29

23. Why does Jessica say she is not buying lipstick?

a. She does not wear lipstick
b. She does not like any of the lipstick colors
c. She wants Amy to buy a lipstick for her
d. The lipstick is expensive, and she is saving her money

24. Which of the following is the best summary of this play?

a. Jessica leaves her other friends to be friends with Amy again, and she and Amy go to the mall
b. Amy teaches Jessica how to steal lipstick without getting caught, being a bad influence on Jessica
c. Jessica agrees to go to the mall with Amy, but when Amy steals lipstick, Jessica goes back to pay for it
d. Jessica thinks stealing is wrong, and she thinks Amy is a bad influence because she is a thief

Questions 25 – 36 pertain to the following two short stories:

THE TALENT SHOW

(1) The first notes floated from the piano. Megan smiled, warm and excited beneath the glaring stage lights. This was her moment. She had practiced. She had prepared. She was ready. As the introduction ended, Megan opened her mouth and began to sing.

(2) The song flowed along, and Megan relaxed, scanning the faces of the audience. But somewhere in the middle of the second verse, her mind suddenly went blank. The music went on, but the words were gone. Megan's smile faded. She stood silently with her mouth hanging open. When the music finally trickled to a stop, Megan ran from the stage.

(3) In a cramped dressing room backstage, Megan buried her face in her hands. She had wanted so much to win this talent show. Tears seeped between her fingers. Her confidence and pride and excitement had been replaced by utter disappointment. She felt a hand on her shoulder and lifted her damp face.

(4) "Ella and Kaylee are here," Megan's mom said, giving her shoulder a quick squeeze.

(5) Ella and Kaylee, Megan's two best friends, pulled folding chairs over to face Megan. She looked at them forlornly.

(6) "I'm a total failure," she moaned.

(7) Ella and Kaylee exchanged glances. Kaylee reached out and squeezed Megan's hand.

(8) "What are you talking about?" Kaylee said. "That first verse was some of your best singing ever."

(9) "Thanks," Megan said. "But the problem is that the first verse is all I sang. Then I totally bombed. I can't believe I forgot the words after all that practice."

(10) "You didn't totally bomb," Ella said. "You just forgot the words. That happens to everybody. Besides, don't the pros say you should leave your audience wanting more?"

(11) "I guess so," Megan admitted.

(12) "Well, trust me," Ella said. "I guarantee they wanted more—like the rest of the song! You probably did, too."

(13) Megan smiled a little. "So, you guys don't think I'm a total dork for forgetting the words?"

(14) "Of course not," Kaylee said. "Forgetting the words doesn't make you a dork. It just makes you human. And you're still the most talented person I know."

(15) Ella nodded in agreement. Megan pulled Ella and Kaylee into a quick hug. Then she wiped her eyes and managed a genuine smile.

18

(16) "I'm so lucky to have best friends like you two," Megan said. "It's nice to know that you'll be my friends forever, no matter what!"

THE TOURNAMENT

(1) Looking for a hole in the defense, Scott dribbled the ball, shifting it from hand to hand. A trickle of sweat ran down his back. No one was open. There were only seconds left on the clock, and Scott knew he had a difficult decision to make.

(2) The other team was leading by two points, and Scott was just outside the three-point line. If he could make the shot, the Eagles would be state champions again. But if he missed ... Scott didn't want to think about that. He knew what he had to do.

(3) It was a classic jump shot. The ball left his hands and sailed toward the basket in a perfect arc. The crowd, the other players, the whole stadium seemed frozen in time. All eyes were on the ball as it struck the rim and bounced off. The buzzer blared. The game was over. Scott had missed, and the Eagles had lost.

(4) Scott stood like a statue on the court as people surged around him. Elated family members swarmed the winning team. Teammates hugged and slapped each other on the back. Even Scott's own teammates joined in the celebration.

(5) Suddenly, Scott felt himself being hoisted unsteadily onto the shoulders of his friends. Over the loudspeaker, the announcer proclaimed that Scott had been named the most valuable player of the championship game. Everyone cheered, and the Eagles took a victory lap with Scott on their shoulders. Finally, Scott's friends put him back on solid ground.

(6) Scott was bewildered. He was the one who missed the most important shot of the game. How could anyone call him the most valuable player? He didn't feel very valuable at the moment. Scott approached Coach Travis.

(7) "Coach," Scott said, "there must be some mistake. I can't be the most valuable player."

(8) "There's no mistake," Coach Travis said. "You had 26 points, 11 rebounds, and 8 assists. I'd say that makes you a very valuable player."

(9) "But I missed that last shot," Scott said. "We lost the game because of me."

(10) "I don't know about that," said Coach Travis. "Everybody misses a shot from time to time. Don't be so hard on yourself. It's all about perspective."

(11) "What do you mean?" Scott asked.

(12) "Well," Coach Travis answered, "you could say you are the reason we lost the game because you missed that last shot. On the other hand, you could say you are the reason we almost won because of your awesome performance throughout the game. How you look at it is up to you."

(13) Scott's teammates came running over and surrounded Coach Travis. They jostled one another playfully, talking and laughing.

(14) "Hey, Coach," one player called out, "how about treating your team to pizza?"

(15) "I don't know," said Coach Travis. "Do you think you deserve pizza?"

(16) Scott piped up. "Of course we do! After all, we almost won the game."

(17) Coach Travis smiled. "You're right, Scott. We did almost win. Okay. Pizza for everyone!"

Questions 25-29 pertain to "The Talent Show" short story:

25. Which of the following is the best definition of "forlornly" as it is used in paragraph 5?
   a. With a happy spirit
   b. With a sad spirit
   c. With a lonely spirit
   d. With an angry spirit

26. What is the main theme of this story?
   a. Real friends support you, no matter what
   b. It is easy to forget the words of a song
   c. Performing in a talent show can be embarrassing
   d. Megan feels like a failure

27. What point of view is used to tell this story?
   a. First person
   b. Second person
   c. Third person
   d. None of the above

28. Which of the following is a supporting detail in this story?
   a. Megan is singing in a talent show
   b. Megan forgets the words of her song
   c. Megan is disappointed in herself
   d. Megan is accompanied by piano music

29. What does Kaylee do in paragraph 8 to try to make Megan feel better?
   a. She makes a joke about Megan's performance
   b. She compliments Megan on her singing
   c. She tells about a time when she forgot a song
   d. She sings a song with Megan

Questions 30-34 pertain to "The Tournament" short story:

30. In paragraph 4, what does "elated" mean?
   a. Happy and excited
   b. Frustrated and angry
   c. Loud and rowdy
   d. Pushy and proud

31. In the first sentence of paragraph 4, what type of figurative language is used?
   a. Hyperbole
   b. Metaphor
   c. Personification
   d. Simile

32. Which of the following best expresses the theme of this story?
   a. The Eagles want to be the state champions
   b. There are different ways to look at any situation
   c. Winning isn't everything
   d. Scott is a very good basketball player

33. Which of the following is the best summary of this story?
   a. At the buzzer, Scott misses an important basket because he isn't a very good basketball player
   b. Coach Travis feels Scott is the most valuable player in the game because he scored 26 points
   c. When Scott misses an important shot, he is disappointed, but Coach Travis shows him there are different ways to look at the situation
   d. The Eagles lose the state championship because of Scott, but Coach Travis sees things differently and makes Scott the most valuable player

34. Why is Scott so upset in this story?
   a. He feels responsible for losing the game
   b. He thinks he is a bad basketball player
   c. He doesn't like Coach Travis
   d. He doesn't want to play basketball anymore

Questions 35-36 pertain to both "The Talent Show" and "The Tournament" short stories:

35. In what ways are Scott and Megan most similar in these stories?
   a. They are both performers.
   b. They are both very active.
   c. They are both disappointed in themselves.
   d. They both have good friends.

36. What general theme is evident in both stories?
   a. Winning is important, but it isn't everything
   b. Good friends are the most valuable thing in life
   c. Coaches can offer good perspective on tough situations
   d. When you try your best, you shouldn't be disappointed in yourself

Questions 37-48 pertain to the following story:

EVERYBODY'S PROBLEM

(1) I used to think homeless people were dirty and lazy and mean. I thought they were all old men with scraggly beards and mangy dogs. I thought they lived on the street because they wanted to. I thought they were all drug addicts and alcoholics who ate from garbage cans and slept in boxes. I used to think homelessness wasn't my problem. Then I met Chris, and he showed me I was wrong—about everything. Homelessness is everybody's problem.

21

(2) The sun was climbing into the bright blue sky as we loaded up the bus at the youth center. It was a crisp, cold Thanksgiving morning, and our youth group was headed down to a local shelter called The Lighthouse. We were going to serve Thanksgiving dinner to more than a hundred homeless people. It seemed like an appropriate way to spend Thanksgiving Day.

(3) When we arrived at the shelter, we were each given a job to do. My job was peeling potatoes. The shelter director gave me a peeler and a garbage can and sat me down in front of a giant pile of potatoes. I had never seen so many potatoes in one place before. They rose from the tray like Mt. Everest. By the time I had peeled them all, my hands and arms and shoulders ached.

(4) When the kitchen work was done, we were given our serving stations. The director explained that this was the only meal many of the homeless people would eat that day, and for some, it was the only hot meal they would have that week. Even so, there wasn't a lot of food for so many people. We were supposed to give each person one slice of turkey, one scoop of mashed potatoes, one scoop of stuffing, a small drizzle of gravy, a few green beans, and a sliver of pumpkin pie.

(5) I was plodding along, dishing up mashed potatoes with an ice cream scoop, when I happened to look up at the person I was serving. He wasn't a dirty, bearded old man. He was a boy about my age, with brown hair and brown eyes and a patched green jacket.

(6) "Hi," the boy said. "I'm Chris."

(7) "I'm Ben," I said as I scooped some potatoes onto his plate. "Happy Thanksgiving."

(8) "Thanks," Chris said, and then he was gone.

(9) As Chris moved down the line, I began to look around, really seeing things for the first time. Very few of the homeless people fit my stereotype. There were men and women, old and young. Children played in a corner of the dining room. At one table, teenagers talked in a tight group. People chatted and smiled. A few were even laughing. This was not what I had pictured a homeless shelter would be like.

(10) When everyone had been served, I began to help clean up. I couldn't help watching Chris as I cleared the tables and wiped them down. He was playing peek-a-boo with a little girl in a high chair. I wondered if it was his little sister.

(11) I was so lost in thought that I jumped when the shelter director tapped my shoulder. She laughed.

(12) "I'll finish cleaning up here," she said. "Why don't you go talk to Chris? He's very nice."

(13) As I approached the table where Chris was sitting, I felt nervous. What would I say? Could we possibly have anything to talk about? Would he even want to talk to me? I sat cautiously beside him.

(14) "Hi, Ben," he said.

(15) "Hi, Chris. Is that your little sister?"

(16) Chris smiled. "Yep. This is Sophia. And over there is my little brother, Dane." Chris motioned toward the corner where the smaller children were playing. Then he pointed to a dark-haired woman at a nearby table. "That's my mom."

(17) "Are you all homeless?" I asked.

(18) "Yep," answered Chris. "We've been here at The Lighthouse for almost two months now. It's okay here, but I miss my old school and my friends. I hope we can move back to a real house soon."

(19) "I didn't know there was such a thing as homeless kids," I admitted.

(20) "Me neither," said Chris. "At least, not until I became one."

(21) "How did it happen?" I asked. Then I had second thoughts. "I mean, you don't have to tell me if you don't want to. I was just wondering."

(22) "It's okay," Chris said. "I don't mind talking about it. About a year ago, my dad got really sick. He was in the hospital for a few months. Then he died. We didn't have any insurance or anything, and my mom couldn't get a job. Besides, she was really sad, and she was trying to take care of me and Dane and Sophia."

(23) "So, how did you end up homeless?" I wondered.

(24) "Mom says there were just too many bills and not enough money. First, we got our lights turned off. Then we couldn't pay our rent, so we had to move out of our house. We stayed with friends for a while, but eventually there was nobody left to stay with. So, we came here."

(25) "Will you stay here forever?" I asked.

(26) "No," Chris said. "My mom is in a program to give her training and help her get a job. When she finds a job, we can get a new place to live. Then things can be normal again."

(27) I heard my youth leader calling for us to load the bus. I wanted to talk to Chris more and ask him more questions, but I knew I had to leave. I stood up.

(28) "I have to go," I said. "I'm glad I got to meet you, Chris. I hope you get a new house soon."

(29) "Thanks, Ben," Chris said. "It was nice to meet you, too. Thanks for hanging out with me for a while. Happy Thanksgiving."

(30) "Happy Thanksgiving," I echoed as I headed toward the door. When I looked back, Chris waved. Then he started playing peek-a-boo with Sophia again.

(31) I will probably never see Chris again, but I have thought of him many times since that day. In just a few minutes together, he taught me so much about the problem of homelessness. It isn't just a problem that affects lazy, mean old men. It affects men and women of all ages. It affects children. It affects whole families. It

affected Chris. And because I got the chance to see homelessness through his eyes, it affects me now, too. I think I'll go back again next Thanksgiving … or maybe sooner. After all, now I know that homelessness is everybody's problem.

37. What is the setting for this story?

a. A youth center
b. A homeless shelter
c. A community center
d. A school

38. If you were describing this story, what classification would you use?

a. Memoir
b. Biography
c. Autobiography
d. Fiction

39. In paragraph 9, what does the word "stereotype" mean?

a. A textbook definition of a concept
b. Height, weight, and physical features
c. A generalized idea of what something is like
d. A description given by an authority figure

40. What point of view is used to tell this story?

a. First person
b. Second person
c. Third person
d. All of the above

41. What is the main theme of this story?

a. Kids can be homeless
b. Potatoes are difficult to peel
c. Serving at a homeless shelter is a good Thanksgiving project
d. Homelessness is everybody's problem

42. What does the author compare the potatoes to in paragraph 3?

a. A tower
b. A mountain range
c. Mt. Everest
d. A mound

43. Which of the following items was not included in the Thanksgiving dinner at the shelter?

a. Turkey
b. Cranberry sauce
c. Mashed potatoes and gravy
d. Pumpkin pie

44. What major event in the life of Chris's family led to their homelessness?

   a.   Their house burned down
   b.   Chris's mom lost her job
   c.   They had to live in their car
   d.   Chris's dad got sick and died

45. How does meeting Chris change Ben's mind about homelessness?

   a.   It doesn't change Ben's mind at all
   b.   It makes Ben afraid of being homeless
   c.   It helps Ben see that homelessness affects everyone
   d.   It keeps Ben from ever helping in a homeless shelter again

46. What do you think the author's primary purpose was in telling this story?

   a.   To persuade the reader to do something about homelessness
   b.   To inform the reader about The Lighthouse homeless shelter
   c.   To educate the reader on Thanksgiving service projects
   d.   To entertain the reader with a story about a personal experience

47. Which of the following is the best summary of this story?

   a.   In the beginning, Ben hates homeless people, but at the end, he loves them
   b.   Ben goes to a homeless shelter to serve Thanksgiving dinner and learns that homelessness affects everyone
   c.   The Lighthouse is a wonderful shelter that serves individuals and families who are homeless
   d.   Ben peels potatoes, serves food, meets Chris, and then goes home

48. Which of the following is Ben most likely to do in the future as a result of meeting Chris at The Lighthouse?

   a.   Avoid homeless people
   b.   Give away all his money
   c.   Try living on the street
   d.   Serve at a homeless shelter again

Written Expression

One of the most important things for you to learn in school is how to express yourself well in written communications. It may seem like being able to write well isn't very important anymore, because so many people communicate via texting and instant messaging these days, and the rules for good writing don't really apply in those forms of communication. While it's true that people don't write as many letters as they used to, it's still necessary to be able to write well. You'll need this skill to do well in school and in college, and in your career once you start working. Improving your writing skills isn't hard; these exercises will help you improve.

Questions 1-8 pertain to the following passage:

An American Hero

(1) In the year 1912, the unsinkable Titanic sank, the United States territory of Arizona became a state, and my Great Uncle Charlie was born. (2) Charlie was born near a small town in Kentucky. (3) On a farm. (4) He grew up learning about the seasons, when to plant the seeds, and when the crops were ripe for picking. (5) His mornings were spent with his hands in dirt as he tended to the growing corps.

(6) When Charlie was only 12, his father died. (7) He had to quit school to take care of his family. (8) While other children were learning and playing at school, Charlie worked in factories to help pay for his mother and sisters to eat. (9) Irregardless of how he felt about having to work, Charlie never complained.

(10) On December 7, 1941, Japan attacked the American naval base at Pearl Harbor. (11) Charlie enlisted in the army when he was 30 years old, and went to fight in the war. (12) He fought in six major battles, including landing in Normandy on D-Day. (13) While he was in the army, Charlie joined the United States horseshoe team and became the champion of the european allies. (14) After the war, Charlie returned to Kentucky married a woman named Bethany, and had three children.

(15) Today, Charlie can still be found with his hands in the dirt. (16) He loves to work in the small garden beside his front porch. (17) The bright colors of ripening strawberries, tomatoes, and ears of corn can be seen next to the house with Charlie walking though the rows of crops with his watering can. (18) He tends to them with love. (19) Charlie watches over his family like the crops in the garden, and that is why he is my hero.

1. What is the BEST way to explain the information in sentences 2 and 3?
   a. Charlie was born near a small town in Kentucky. It was on a farm.
   b. Charlie was born in Kentucky. Near a small town and on a farm.
   c. Charlie was born near a small town. In Kentucky, it was on a farm.
   d. Charlie was born on a farm near a small Kentucky town.

2. What change, if any, should be made to sentence 5?
   a. Change *corps* to *crops*
   b. Change *were* to *was*
   c. Insert a comma after *dirt*
   d. Make no change

3. What change, if any, should be made to sentence 9?

   a. Change *complained* to *complains*
   b. Change *irregardless* to *regardless*
   c. Delete the comma after *work*
   d. Make no change

4. What sentence could BEST follow and support sentence 10?

   a. Pearl Harbor is a naval base in Hawaii
   b. The USS Arizona was one of the battleships that sank
   c. This event directly led into the United States' involvement in World War II
   d. Charlie had never been to Hawaii

5. What change, if any, should be made to sentence 13?

   a. Change *european* to *European*
   b. Change *became* to *becomes*
   c. Insert a comma after *champion*
   d. Make no change

6. What change, if any, should be made to sentence 14?

   a. Change *returned* to *returns*
   b. Insert a comma after *Kentucky*
   c. Insert *and* after *Kentucky*
   d. Make no change

7. What change, if any, should be made in sentence 16?

   a. Change *loves* to *loved*
   b. Insert a comma after *garden*
   c. Change *beside* to *besides*
   d. Make no change

8. What change, if any, should be made in sentence 17?

   a. Change *colors* to *colours*
   b. Delete the comma after *strawberries*
   c. Change *though* to *through*
   d. Make no change

Questions 9 – 16 pertain to the following story:

The Top Deck

(1) We walked outside through the sliding glass doors and waited in line for the large, double-decker red bus. (2) My family flew to London for a week in July to celebrate my sisters graduation. (3) She wore a blue cap and gown. (4) The sky was gray, and light puddles spotted the ground. (5) As the bus pulled up against the curb, dirty water splashed our feet.

(6) The driver's seat was on the opposite side of the bus, and the driver smiled at me when I showed him my ticket. (7) I looked out the window and realised that we were driving on the opposite side of the street. (8) All around us people who were on the wrong side of the street driving from what looked like the passenger seat. (9) The bus

was filled with people. (10) Almost every seat was taken, and people were even standing in the aisle holding onto handrails and poles. (11) Their was a spiral staircase directly behind the driver, and we walked up it to try and find more seats. (12) There were two rows of seats upstairs and a large window that looked onto the streets. (13) For seats were open near the front of the bus and we hurried to get them.

(14) The bus stopped every few seconds, and each time I had to hold onto my seat to keep from sliding into the aisle. (15) "What street are we looking for?" my dad asked my mom. (16) "Oxford" she replied. (17) I looked out the giant window. (18) We passed a large building that was shaped like an egg, and we continued to travel. (19) The bus driver's voice came over the speakers. (20) "Now approaching Liverpool," he said

(21) My mom looked at my dad. (22) I grabbed my sister's arm, but she was busy taking pictures of the buildings out the window. (23) "Liverpool," my mom whispered with a worried look on her face. (24) "We're lost, aren't we?" my dad said.

9. What change, if any, should be made in sentence 2?
   a. Change *flew* to *flied*
   b. Change *week* to *weak*
   c. Change *sisters* to *sister's*
   d. Make no change

10. What change, if any, should be made in sentence 7?
   a. Change *realised* to *realize*
   b. Change *street* to *streat*
   c. Change *looked* to *look*
   d. Make no change

11. What change, if any, should be made in sentence 11?
   a. Delete the comma after *driver*
   b. Change *Their* to *There*
   c. Change *staircase* to *stair case*
   d. Make no change

12. What change should be made in sentence 13?
   a. Change *open* to *opened*
   b. Change *were* to *was*
   c. Change *For* to *Four*
   d. Change *hurried* to *hurried*

13. Which of the following is the BEST way to rewrite the ideas in sentence 8?
   a. All around us people were driving from what looked like the passenger seat, and they were driving on the opposite side of the street
   b. All around us people who were on the wrong side of the street, driving from what looked like the passenger seat
   c. All around us people were driving on the wrong side of the street. Driving from what looked like the passenger seat
   d. All around us people were driving from what looked like passenger seat, they were on the opposite side of the street

28

14. What change, if any, should be made in sentence 16?

a. Change *Oxford* to *oxford*
b. Insert a comma after *Oxford*
c. Insert a period after the quotation mark
d. Make no change

15. Which sentence does not belong in this essay?

a. Sentence 20
b. Sentence 6
c. Sentence 13
d. Sentence 3

16. What is the BEST transition word or phrase that could be added to the beginning of sentence 19?

a. However
b. Once in a while
c. Additionally
d. After a while

Questions 17 -24 pertain to the following story:

Longhorn Café

(1) Last Saturday night my dad took me to watch the Longhorns play football in Austin. (2) It was a cool evening, and the orange-painted stadium was filled with screaming fans. (3) Even though we live in San Antonio, my dad has always been a dedicated Longhorns fan, and he wears his orange proudly.

(4) We arrived in Austin early. (5) "Traffic," my dad said as his only explanation. (6) He parked the truck down a small side street and motions for me to get out and follow him. (7) "I want to take you someplace," he said. (8) "I used to come here all the time when I was in college. (9) We walked up to a small building with a large patio off to the side. (10) A large tree with low branches spread across the patio and connected with the roof. (11) The leaves were beginning to change colors, and it was like sitting under a leafy canopy.

(12) We sat at a table outside on a rusting rocking bench beside an abandoned bathtub. (13) Stands of colored lights hung across the patio. (14) Wrapped around the tree. (15) "What is this place?" I asked. (16) My dad smiled and pointed to a sign bordered with colored lights. (17) "Spider Café," he said. (18) All around us, people were drinking coffee and staring at them computer screens. (19) Our waiter was named Chris, and he had a long beard, wore a dirtied apron, and carried empty coffee mugs.

(20) The waited came up to us, and my dad ordered himself a latte and a sweet drink for me. (21) My dad looked around the patio and smiled. (22) He leaned into the bench and placed his hand on the side of the bathtub. (23) He didn't even mind when he spilled coffee onto his favorite orange shirt. (24) "You'll love it here," he said, "when you are a Longhorn football player?"

17. What change, if any, should be made in sentence 5?

a. Delete the comma after *traffic*
b. Insert a comma after *said*
c. Change *said* to *says*
d. Make no change

18. What change should be made in sentence 6?

a. Change *parked* to *park*
b. Change *street* to *Street*
c. Insert a comma after *street*
d. Change *motions* to *motioned*

19. What change, if any, should be made in sentence 8?

a. Change *come* to *came*
b. Change *to* to *too*
c. Insert a quotation mark after *college*
d. Make no change

20. What revision, if any, is needed in sentences 13 and 14?

a. Strands of colored lights hung across the patio wrapped, around the tree
b. Strands of colored lights hung across the patio and wrapped around the tree
c. Strands of colored lights hung. Across the patio, wrapped around the tree
d. No revision is needed

21. What change, if any, should be made in sentence 18?

a. Change *them* to *their*
b. Delete the comma after *us*
c. Insert a comma after *and*
d. Make no change

22. Where is the best placement for sentence 19?

a. After sentence 22
b. After sentence 20
c. Before sentence 18
d. No change is needed

23. What change, if any, should be made in sentence 20?

a. Change *ordered* to *orders*
b. Change *himself* to *hisself*
c. Change *waited* to *waiter*
d. Make no change

24. What change should be made in sentence 24?

a. Change *Longhorn* to *longhorn*
b. Change *you are* to *your*
c. Change *football* to *Football*
d. Change the question mark to a period

30

Questions 25 – 32 pertain to the following story:

Strike Three

(1) As I stared down at the hitter in the batters box, I remembered what my dad had said to me. (2) "Shut everything out." (3) I focused on the glove in front of me. (4) I looked into the deep, blackened pocket, and sawed my target. (5) The batter tapped his bat against the sides of his cleats, and rested the bat on his shoulders. (6) With hard eyes, he stares back at me.

(7) I kicked the front of my cleat into the bright white rubber on the pitching mound and took a deep breath. (8) Shut everything out," he had said. (9) Slowly the noises disappeared. (10) I could no longer hear the shouts from the parents in the stands. (11) In my head, I silenced the cheers from both dugouts. (12) The umpire did not exist. (13) There were no players, no coaches, not even a catcher. (14) There was just me. (15) The ball and the glove.

(16) I took a deep breath and brought my hands together at my chest. (17) I looked over at first base, but there was no runner. (18) In one motion, my feet left the rubber and connected with ground. (19) Dirt flew in the air as my arm rotated forward and released the ball in front of me. (20) I watched as the ball spun and landed into glove with a hard crack. (21) The umpire shot up from his crouched position and pointed his finger to the right and yelled, "Strike Three!"

(22) The noises came back. (23) The crowd cheered in the stands and I could here stomping feet. (24) My teammate clapped his hand to its glove and ran toward me. (25) My coach raised a first into the air in celebration. (26) I was surrounded by my teammates, and they were patting me on the back. (27) My dad was sitting on a bleacher behind home plate. (28) He raised his thumb to me and smiled as I ran off the field with my teammates.

25. What change, if any, should be made in sentence 1?
   a. Change *stared* to *starred*
   b. Change *dad* to *Dad*
   c. Change *batters* to *batter's*
   d. Make no change

26. What change should be made in sentence 4?
   a. Change *blackened* to *blacked*
   b. Change *sawed* to *saw*
   c. Delete the comma after *deep*
   d. Change *into* to *in to*

27. What change, if any, should be made in sentence 6?
   a. Change *stares* to *stared*.
   b. Change *me* to *I*
   c. Delete the comma after *eyes*
   d. Make no change

28. What change should be made in sentence 8?

a. Change *everything* to *every thing*
b. Delete the comma after *out*
c. Change the comma after *out* to a period
d. Insert quotation marks before *Shut*

29. What is the best way to combine sentence 14 and sentence 15?

a. There was just the ball, the glove, and me
b. There was just me, the ball, and the glove
c. There was just me and the ball and the glove
d. Make no change

30. What change, if any, should be made in sentence 23?

a. Change *cheered* to *cheer*
b. Change *here* to *hear*
c. Change *could* to *can*
d. Make no change

31. What sentence could BEST follow and support sentence 22?

a. My foot was still planted hard into the ground
b. The sounds came flooding into my ears as I looked up
c. I felt good
d. The umpire took off his mask and started walking toward the fence

32. What is the BEST transition word that could be added to the beginning of sentence 26?

a. However
b. Consequentially
c. Soon
d. Therefore

Questions 33 – 40 pertain to the following passage:

Imagine a Better World

(1) My favorite song is "imagine" by John Lennon. (2) It was released in 1971. (3) It is one of the few famous songs that John Lennon recorded and sang alone. (4) For the majority of his career, John Lennon was a member of an iconic rock band called the Beatles, a band that changed the music industry. (5) The Beatles accepted a lot of success in their career, with popular songs such as "I Want to Hold Your Hand," "Come Together," "Let it Be," and "Here Comes the Sun." (6) After the band decided to separate, John Lennon became a solo artist as well as an promoter for peace.

(7) "Imagine" tells the story of Lennons dream of peace in the world. He asks the listener to imagine different situations. (8) He says to imagine that there are no countries, religions, or possessions. (9) He says, "I wonder if you can." (10) This line strikes me the most I try to imagine such a world. (11) When talking about no possessions, he continues and says, "No need for greed or hunger." (12) It is a great line. (13) Throughout the song, he says, "Imagine all the people." (14) And he gives examples. (15) At first he says, "living for today," and then moves on to say, "living life in peace," and finally, "sharing all the world."

(16) My favorite part of the song is the chorus. (17) Lennon says, "You may say I'm a dreamer, but I'm not the only one. (18) I hope someday you'll join us, and the world will be as one." (19) When I really listen to the words of this song, I realize that "Imagine" is so much more than something that sounds nicely. (20) Lennon is saying something very important and suggesting ways in which the world can live in peace. (21) Because of this song, I am a dreamer as well, and I join John Lennon in the fight for world peace.

33. What change, if any, should be made in sentence 1?

a. Change *favorite* to *favourite*
b. Change *imagine* to *Imagine*
c. Insert a comma after *song*
d. Make no change

34. What is the BEST verb to replace *accepted* in sentence 5?

a. Lasted
b. Liked
c. Had
d. Watched

35. What change should be made in sentence 6?

a. Change *separate* to *separated*
b. Insert a comma after *artist*
c. Change *solo* to *Solo*
d. Change *an* to *a*

36. What change, if any, should be made in sentence 7?

a. Change *Lennons* to *Lennon's*
b. Change *dream* to *dreamt*
c. Insert a comma after *peace*
d. Make no change

37. What is the BEST way to revise sentence 10?

a. This line strikes me the most as I try to imagine such a world.
b. This line strikes me the most, I try to imagine such a world.
c. This line strikes me, the most. I try to imagine such a world.
d. No revision needed.

38. What is the BEST way to combine sentence 13 and sentence 14?

a. Throughout the song, he says "Imagine all the people" and he gives examples.
b. Throughout the song, he says, "Imagine all the people," and he gives examples.
c. Throughout the song he says Imagine all the people, and he gives examples.
d. Throughout the song he says Imagine all the people and he gives examples.

39. What change, if any, should be made in sentence 18?

a. Insert a quotation mark before *I*
b. Move the period after the quotation marks
c. Change *you'll* to *youl'l*
d. Make no change

40. What change should be made in sentence 19?

    a.   Delete the comma after *song*

    b.   Change *something* to *some thing*

    c.   Change *nicely* to *nice*

    d.   Change *realize* to *realized*

Mathematics

Did you ever stop to think about the fact that almost everything in life involves math? This might sound unbelievable at first, but it's true. Without math, there would be no way to have sports, or video games, or TV, or the internet, or movies, or anything else. There would be no houses, no furniture, no cars, or anything else that's manmade, because you have to use math to build everything. There would be no music, either, because math is at the very heart of music.

So, don't ever let anyone tell you that math is boring. It's actually the exact opposite. It's not only a necessary part of every aspect of life, it's also fascinating. Whenever you run into a math problem you're having difficulty with, just think of it as a puzzle you need to solve. Here are some math questions that can help you improve your skills in this area.

1. Antonio wants to buy a roll of border to finish an art project. At four different shops, he found four different borders he liked. He wants to use the widest of the borders. The list shows the width, in inches, of the borders he found.

$$1\frac{7}{10}, 1.72, 1\frac{3}{4}, 1.695$$

Which roll of border should Antonio buy if he wants to buy the widest border?

a. $1\frac{7}{10}$
b. 1.72
c. $1\frac{3}{4}$
d. 1.695

2. Daniella wrote a decimal and a fraction which were equivalent to each other. Which pair of numbers could be the pair Daniella wrote?

a. $0.625, \frac{7}{8}$
b. $0.375, \frac{3}{8}$
c. $0.75, \frac{7}{5}$
d. $0.45, \frac{4}{5}$

3. Glenda poured salt into three salt shakers from a box that contained 26 ounces of salt. She poured 2 ounces of salt into one shaker, 3 ounces of salt into the second shaker, and 4 ounces into the third shaker. She did not pour salt into any other shakers. Which expression best represents the amount of salt left in the box after Glenda poured salt into the three shakers?

a. $2 - 3 - 4 + 26$
b. $2 + 3 + 4 - 26$
c. $26 - 2 + 3 + 4$
d. $26 - 2 - 3 - 4$

4. Which expression best shows the prime factorization of 750?

a. $2 \times 3 \times 5^3$
b. $2 \times 3 \times 5^2$
c. $2 \times 3 \times 5 \times 25$
d. $2 \times 3 \times 5^2 \times 25$

5. The drawing shows a window with equal-sized panes. Some of the panes are not tinted, some are tinted a light shade of gray, and some are tinted a very dark shade of gray.

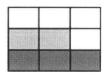

Which number sentence best models the total section of the window that has tinted panes?

a. $\frac{1}{3} + \frac{1}{3} = \frac{2}{3}$

b. $\frac{1}{3} + \frac{2}{9} = \frac{5}{9}$

c. $\frac{1}{9} + \frac{2}{3} = \frac{7}{9}$

d. $\frac{2}{9} + \frac{4}{9} = \frac{2}{3}$

6. Julie shopped for first-aid cream. One large tube held 1.5 fluid ounces and the smallest tube held 0.33 fluid ounces. What is the difference in the number of fluid ounces of cream in the two tubes?

a. 1.8

b. 1.27

c. 1.23

d. 1.17

7. Large boxes of canned beans hold 24 cans of beans and small boxes hold 12 cans. One afternoon, Gerald brought 4 large boxes of canned beans and 6 small boxes of canned beans to the food bank. How many cans of beans did Gerald bring to the food bank that afternoon?

a. 168

b. 192

c. 288

d. 360

8. Jeff saw 25 cars in the school parking lot. If each car brought from 1 to 3 people to school, which is the best estimate of the total number of people arriving to school in the 25 cars?

a. 25

b. 50

c. 75

d. 100

9. Enrique used a formula to find the total cost, in dollars, for repairs he and his helper, Jenny, made to a furnace. The expression below shows the formula he used, with 4 being the number of hours he worked on the furnace and 2 being the number of hours Jenny worked on the furnace.

$$20 + 35(4 + 2) + 47$$

What is the total cost for repairing the furnace?

a. $189

b. $269

c. $277

d. $377

10. One morning at Jim's café, 25 people ordered juice, 10 ordered milk, and 50 ordered coffee with breakfast. Which ratio best compares the number of people who ordered milk to the number of people who ordered juice?

    a. 5 to 7
    b. 5 to 2
    c. 2 to 7
    d. 2 to 5

11. At the middle school Vanessa attends, there are 240 Grade 6 students, 210 Grade 7 students, and 200 Grade 8 students. Which ratio best compares the number of students in Grade 8 to the number of students in Grade 6 at Vanessa's school?

    a. 5 : 6
    b. 5 : 11
    c. 6 : 5
    d. 7 : 8

12. A display at the bottom of the laptop computer Erica was using showed that the battery had a 70% charge. Which decimal is equivalent to 70%?

    a. 0.07
    b. 70.0
    c. 7.0
    d. 0.7

13. The drawing shows a chart used to record completed Math assignments. A checkmark is used to show which assignments are finished.

Math Assignment

✓	✓	✓	✓	✓
✓	✓	✓	✓	✓
✓	✓	✓		
✓	✓			

Which of the following shows the percentage of Math assignments in the chart which are finished?

    a. 15%
    b. 25%
    c. 55%
    d. 75%

14. Harold learned that 6 out of 10 students at his school live within two miles of the school. If 240 students attend Grade 6 at his school, about how many of these students should Harold expect to live within two miles of the school?

    a. 24
    b. 40
    c. 144
    d. 180

15. A unit of liquid measure in the English System of Measure is the gill. The table, shown here, gives conversions from gills to fluid ounces.

Conversion Table

Gills	Fluid Ounces
2	8
4	16
5	20
6	24
10	40

Which equation best describes the relationship between gills, g, and fluid ounces, f?

a. $f = 8g - 8$
b. $f = 2g + 4$
c. $f = 4g$
d. $4f = g$

16. The table below shows changes in the area of several trapezoids as the lengths of the bases, b_1 and b_2, remain the same and the height, h, changes.

Trapezoids

b_1 (in feet)	b_2 (in feet)	h (in feet)	A (in square feet)
5	7	2	12
5	7	4	24
5	7	6	36
5	7	8	48

Which formula best represents the relationship between A, the areas of these trapezoids, and h, their heights?

a. $A = 5h$
b. $A = 6h$
c. $A = 7h$
d. $A = 12h$

17. A trash company charges a fee of $80 to haul off a load of trash. There is also a charge of $0.05 per mile the load must be hauled. Which equation can be used to find c, the cost for hauling a load of trash m miles?

a. $80(m + 0.05)$
b. $0.05(m + 80)$
c. $80m + 0.05$
d. $0.05m + 80$

18. This table shows lengths, widths, and areas of four rectangles. In each rectangle, the length remains 40 meters, but the width changes.

Rectangles				
Length	40 meters	40 meters	40 meters	40 meters
Width	20 meters	30 meters	40 meters	50 meters
Perimeter	120 meters	140 meters	160 meters	180 meters

Which formula best represents the relationship between _P_, the perimeters of these rectangles, and _w_, their widths?

- a. $P = w + 80$
- b. $P = 2w + 80$
- c. $P = 2(2w + 40)$
- d. $P = 10(w + 40)$

19. Thomas drew a polygon with vertices: _A_, _B_, _C_, and _D_. He measured the angles formed and recorded the information shown here.

$$m\angle A = 70°, m\angle B = 80°, m\angle C = 120°, m\angle D = 90°$$

Which of the angles that Thomas drew is an obtuse angle?

- a. $\angle A$
- b. $\angle B$
- c. $\angle C$
- d. $\angle D$

20. Georgia measured and labeled the angles shown in this drawing.

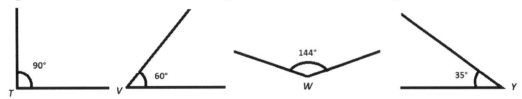

Which of the angles that Georgia measured is a right angle?

- a. $\angle T$
- b. $\angle V$
- c. $\angle W$
- d. $\angle Y$

21. In ΔRST, shown here, m∠S is 20° less than m∠R.

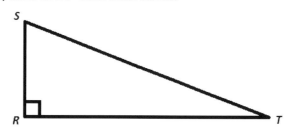

What is the measure of ∠T?

    a. 110°
    b. 70°
    c. 50°
    d. 20°

22. Ellen measured ∠R in the parallelogram shown here and found it to be 35°. She knows that ∠R and ∠T have equal measures. She also knows ∠S and ∠V are equal in measure.

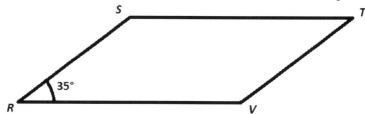

What is the measure of ∠V?

    a. 215°
    b. 145°
    c. 70°
    d. 35°

23. A worker put 2 strings of lights around a circular pond in the city park, so that each string of lights went around the entire pond once. The total length of the strings of lights was 100 feet. Which expression, when used by itself, can be used to determine the distance across the center of the pond?

    a. $100 \div \pi$
    b. $\pi \div 100$
    c. $(100 \div 2) \div \pi$
    d. $(\pi \div 100) \div 2$

40

24. Omar drew a circle on paper by carefully tracing completely around the outside of a CD from a computer game. He measured across the center of the CD and found the distance to be 12 centimeters.

Which expression can be used to find the distance, in centimeters, around the circle Omar made?

   a. $12(\pi)$
   b. $2(12)(\pi)$
   c. $(12 \div 2)(\pi)$
   d. $2(\pi \div 12)$

25. Use this grid to answer the question.

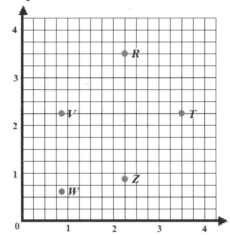

Which ordered pair best represents the coordinates of Point R?

   a. $(2\frac{1}{4}, 3\frac{1}{2})$
   b. $(3\frac{1}{2}, 2\frac{1}{4})$
   c. $(9, 14)$
   d. $(14, 9)$

26. The tires on Ginny's bike are about 20 inches from the top of the tire to the ground. Which of these is closest to the distance around each tire?

   a. 60 inches
   b. 180 inches
   c. 400 inches
   d. 1,200 inches

27. Jessica wrote down the times required for five girls to run a race. The times are shown in this list.

25.1 seconds, 24.9 seconds, 25.2 seconds, 24.8 seconds, 25.0 seconds

What time is closest to the total for all five runners?

a. 1 minute and 5 seconds
b. 1 minute and 25 seconds
c. 2 minutes and 5 seconds
d 2 minutes and 25 seconds

28. **This drawing shows an equilateral triangle and a ruler.**

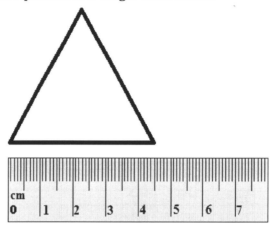

Which is closest to the perimeter of the triangle?

a. 4.5 centimeters
b. 9.0 centimeters
c. 13.5 centimeters
d. 20.3 centimeters

29. **The drawing shows a protractor and a trapezoid.**

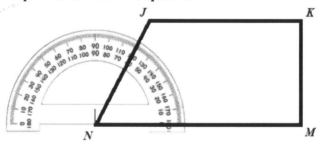

Which is closest to the measure of ∠JNM?

a. 61°
b. 79°
c. 119°
d. 121°

30. The length of the football field near Gerald's school is 120 yards. What is the length of the field in feet?

    a. 1,440 feet
    b. 360 feet
    c. 400 feet
    d. 12 feet

31. Jan played a game which used a fair spinner like the one shown here. Jan needs the arrow to land on green on her next turn.

What is the probability that the arrow lands on green when Jan spins one time?

    a. $\frac{1}{6}$
    b. $\frac{1}{3}$
    c. $\frac{1}{2}$
    d. $\frac{2}{3}$

32. Hillside Middle School students are choosing school colors from three dark colors (black, blue, and brown) and two light colors (white and yellow). Which tree diagram best shows all possible color combinations of one dark color and one light color?

    a.

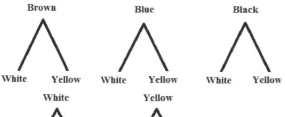

    b.

    c.

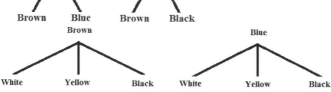

    d.

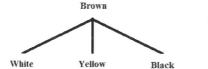

33. Stephen researched the topic of solar-powered lights for his science project. He exposed 10 new solar lights to five hours of sunlight. He recorded the number of minutes each light continued to shine after dark in the list below.

63, 67, 73, 75, 80, 91, 63, 72, 79, 87

Which of these numbers is the mean of the number of minutes in Stephen's list?

    a.   28
    b.   63
    c.   74
    d.   75

34. Grade 6 students at Fairview Middle School were asked to name their favorite of six school subjects. The plot below shows a summary of their answers. Each X represents 5 students.

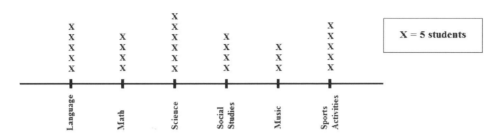

Which graph best represents the data in the plot?

a.

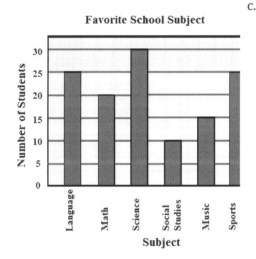

c.

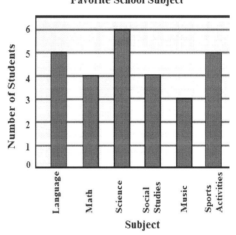

b.

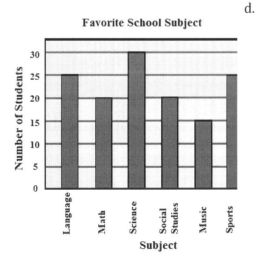

d.

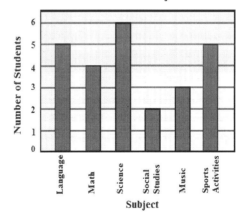

35. Sammie had $120 he had earned doing chores for people in his neighborhood. When school started, he spent $50 for shirts, $30 for jeans, and $40 for school supplies. Which graph best represents how Sammy spent his $120?

a.

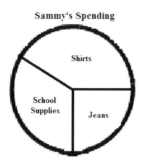

c.

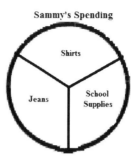

b.

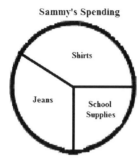

d.

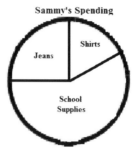

36. James and his driving partner, Larissa, recently drove a truck from Dallas, TX to Los Angeles, CA. The total distance they drove was 1,380 miles. James is paid $0.35 per mile he drives and Larissa is paid $0.30 per mile she drives. What additional information is needed to find the amount James should be paid for the trip?

    a. The total number of hours each person drove
    b. The total number of miles each person drove
    c. The total amount of fuel the truck used
    d. The total weight of the truck and cargo

37. Petra installed 10 light fixtures at a new warehouse that was being built. Each of the fixtures required 3 light bulbs. The bulbs come in packages of 5 and cost $8 per package. What was the total cost for the bulbs required for all of the fixtures Petra installed at the warehouse?

    a. $16
    b. $48
    c. $120
    d. $240

38. Anna and other members of her club sold caps to commemorate their city's 100ᵗʰ birthday. The caps sold for $14 and came in four colors. The club made $3,360 in total sales from selling the caps. The graph below shows the part of the total sales that each color represented.

Colors of Caps Sold

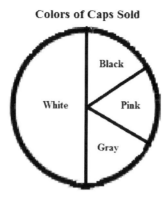

Which number is closest to the combined number of white and pink caps sold by Anna's club members?

    a. 40
    b. 80
    c. 120
    d. 160

39. Some wind generators have blades that look like propellers. When the wind blows, these blades turn in a circle and make electricity. One type has blades that are 100 feet long. If the blades on this type of wind generator turn 15 times each minute, what would be a reasonable distance for the blade tip to travel in 1 minute?

    a. 1,500 feet
    b. 3,000 feet
    c. 4,500 feet
    d. 9,000 feet

40. Jason wants to put dry fertilizer on the grass in his front yard. The yard is 20 feet wide and 45 feet long. Each pound of the fertilizer he plans to use is enough for 150 square feet. Which procedure could Jason use to determine the correct amount of fertilizer to use on the entire yard?

    a. Divide 150 by 20 and divide 150 by 45, and then add those quotients together
    b. Add 20 and 45, double that total, and then divide that total by 150
    c. Multiply 20 by 45, and then subtract 150 from that product
    d. Multiply 20 by 45, and then divide that product by 150

41. Tomas needs $100 to buy a telescope he wants. He received $40 as a gift and spent $10 on a book about telescopes. He earned $35 doing small jobs for his family. The steps Tomas can use to find the amount he still needs to save to buy the telescope are shown here in incorrect order.

Step R: Subtract 65 from 100.
Step S: Subtract 10 from 40.
Step T: Add 35 to 30.

Which sequence shows the steps in the correct order?

a. T, S, R
b. T, R, S
c. S, T, R
d. R, S, T

42. The repeating pattern shown below uses the same four figures over and over again.

Fig. 1   Fig. 2   Fig. 3   Fig. 4   Fig. 5   Fig. 6 ...

Which of the four figures will the figure in the 31st position look like?

a. Figure 1
b. Figure 2
c. Figure 3
d. Figure 4

43. Two sets of numbers are shown here. In each set, the terms increase by the same amount each time.

Set M = {1, 4, 7, 10, 13, ...}

Set V = {1, 3, 5, 7, 9, ...}

What is the first number greater than 20 which is a member of both Set M and Set V?

a. 21
b. 23
c. 25
d. 27

44. Antoinette had $50 she had saved. At a craft show, she bought 2 pairs of earrings for $10 each and a picture for $12. She also spent $7 on lunch. If she spent no other money, how much money should Antoinette have left from the $50?

a. $35, because $50 − (10 +12) + 7 = 35$
b. $25, because $50 − [2(10) +12] + 7 = 25$
c. $21, because $50 − (10 + 12 + 7) = 21$
d. $11, because $50 − [2(10) + 12 +7] = 11$

45. Candace's shoelace broke. She measured the unbroken shoelace and finds that she needs a replacement lace that is at least 16 inches long. The store has the following lengths available.

$$15\frac{7}{10}, 16.25, \frac{47}{3}, 15.5$$

Which one of the following lace lengths would be long enough to replace the broken shoelace?

    a. $15\frac{7}{10}$
    b. 16.25
    c. $\frac{47}{3}$
    d. 15.5

46. Nadia is working summer jobs. She earns $5 for every dog she walks, $2 for bringing back a trashcan, $1 for checking the mail, and $5 for watering the flowers. Nadia walks 3 dogs, brings back 5 trashcans, checks the mail for 10 neighbors, and waters the flowers at 6 houses. Which expression can be used to find out how much money Nadia earned?

    a. $2(5) + $6(10) + $1
    b. $10(6) + $1 + $5
    c. $5(3+6) + $2(5) + $1(10)
    d. $15 + $10 + $16

47. Only 8% of the dogs were solid white. Which decimal is equivalent to 8%?

    a. 0.08
    b. 80.0
    c. 8.0
    d. 0.8

48. Use this grid to answer the question.

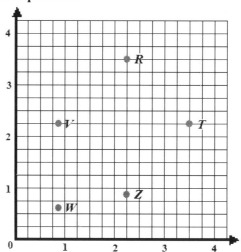

Which of the points on the grid best represents the point at $(2\frac{1}{4}, \frac{7}{8})$?

    a.   T
    b.   V
    c.   W
    d.   Z

49. Four students measured the length of the pencil each was using. The list shows the lengths, in centimeters, of the four pencils.

    17.03 cm, 17.4 cm, 17.31 cm, 17.09 cm

Which list shows the lengths of the pencils in order, from shortest to longest?

    a.   17.4 cm, 17.31 cm, 17.09 cm, 17.03 cm
    b.   17.03 cm, 17.09 cm, 17.4 cm, 17.31 cm
    c.   17.4 cm, 17.03 cm, 17.09 cm, 17.31 cm
    d.   17.03 cm, 17.09 cm, 17.31 cm, 17.4 cm

50. Castor collects only baseball and football cards. He has 40 baseball cards and 10 football cards. Which decimal best shows the part of his entire card collection represented by his baseball cards?

    a.   0.8
    b.   0.75
    c.   0.4
    d.   0.25

51. Which expression best shows the prime factorization of 630?

    a. $2 \times 3 \times 105$
    b. $2 \times 5 \times 7 \times 9$
    c. $2 \times 3^2 \times 5 \times 7$
    d. $2^2 \times 3^2 \times 5 \times 7$

52. A club is making necklaces in school colors. They plan to use an equal number of blue beads and silver beads on each necklace. The blue beads come in bags of 60 and the silver beads come in bags of 80. What is the smallest number of bags of each color the club can purchase to have an equal number of each color bead with no beads left when the necklaces are finished?

    a. 3 bags of blue and 4 bags of silver
    b. 4 bags of blue and 3 bags of silver
    c. 40 bags of blue and 30 bags of silver
    d. 80 bags of blue and 60 bags of silver

53. Olga drew the regular figure shown here. She painted part of the figure a light color and part of it a darker color. She left the rest of the figure white.

Which of the following equations best models the part of the figure Olga left white?

    a. $1 - \frac{1}{3} - \frac{1}{3} = \frac{1}{3}$
    b. $1 - \frac{1}{6} - \frac{1}{6} = \frac{2}{3}$
    c. $1 - \frac{1}{6} - \frac{1}{2} = \frac{1}{3}$
    d. $1 - \frac{1}{2} - \frac{1}{3} = \frac{2}{3}$

54. Evan measured the amount of rain in the gauge over the weekend. On Saturday, he measured $1\frac{6}{10}$ inches and on Sunday, $\frac{8}{10}$ inches. What is the total amount of rain, in inches, Evan measured on those two days, written in the simplest form?

    a. $1\frac{14}{20}$
    b. $1\frac{4}{10}$
    c. $1\frac{2}{5}$
    d. $2\frac{2}{5}$

55. Rafael purchased 8 new tires for the two family cars. The price of each tire was $144, including taxes. He agreed to make 18 equal monthly payments, interest-free, to pay for the tires. What will be the amount Rafael should pay each month?

    a. $16
    b. $32
    c. $64
    d. $128

56. A farmer had about 150 bags of potatoes on his trailer. Each bag contained from 23 to 27 pounds of potatoes. Which is the best estimate of the total number of pounds of potatoes on the farmer's trailer?

    a.   3,000
    b.   3,700
    c.   4,100
    d.   5,000

57. William needs to find the value of the expression below. What is the value of this expression?

$$40 - 4(3 - 1)$$

    a.   29
    b.   32
    c.   72
    d.   107

58. Elena counted the number of birds that came to her bird bath one afternoon. While she watched, 20 sparrows, 16 finches, 4 wrens, and 10 jays came to the bird bath. Which ratio, in simplest form, compares the number of finches that Elena counted to the number of sparrows?

    a.   4 : 5
    b.   4 : 9
    c.   16 : 20
    d.   20 : 36

59. One cold afternoon at a small café, 20 people drank hot tea, 45 drank coffee, and 15 drank hot chocolate. Which ratio compares the number of people who drank coffee to the number who drank tea?

    a.   4 to 13
    b.   4 to 9
    c.   9 to 4
    d.   3 to 1

60. A lake near Armando's home is reported to be 80% full of water. Which fraction is equivalent to 80% and in simplest form?

    a. $\dfrac{1}{80}$
    b. $\dfrac{8}{10}$
    c. $\dfrac{4}{5}$
    d. $\dfrac{80}{1}$

61. The rectangle in this drawing is divided into equal-sized parts, with some of them shaded a darker color.

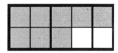

What percent best represents the part of the rectangle that is shaded a darker color?

    a. 8%
    b. 20%
    c. 53%
    d. 80%

62. Annette read that out of 20 televisions sold in her state last year, 3 were Brand V. If a furniture store near her home sold 360 televisions last year, about how many should Annette expect to be Brand V?

    a. 18
    b. 54
    c. 1,080
    d. 2,400

63. The table below gives the positions of several terms in a sequence and the values of those terms.

Sequence

Position of term, n	Value of Term
1	1
2	6
3	11
4	16
5	21
n	?

Which rule can be used to find the value of n?

    a. 5n
    b. 6n
    c. $5n - 4$
    d. $6n - 5$

64. Julia has a cell phone contract with a monthly charge of $45. She bought a phone with a one-time price of $50 with that contract. Which table best represents the total of all charges which should be paid at the end of each month of the contract?

a.

Number of Months	1	2	3	4	5	6
Total Charges	$45	$90	$135	$180	$225	$270

b.

Number of Months	1	2	3	4	5	6
Total Charges	$95	$140	$185	$230	$275	$320

c.

Number of Months	1	2	3	4	5	6
Total Charges	$95	$190	$285	$380	$475	$570

d.

Number of Months	1	2	3	4	5	6
Total Charges	$50	$95	$140	$185	$230	$275

65. This table shows bases, heights, and areas of four triangles. In each triangle, the base remains the same and the height changes.

Triangles				
Base, *b*	30 yards	30 yards	30 yards	30 yards
Height, *h*	20 yards	40 yards	60 yards	80 yards
Area, *A*	300 square yards	600 square yards	900 square yards	1200 square yards

Which formula best represents the relationship between *A*, the areas of these triangles, and *h*, their heights?

    a. $A = \dfrac{h}{30}$

    b. $A = \dfrac{h}{15}$

    c. $A = 30h$

    d. $A = 15h$

These exercises and problems will help you in your math classes. You'll solve problems involving addition, subtraction, division, multiplication, decimals, geometry, shapes, and graphs. You'll find a lot of helpful instructions along the way. Take your time and do your best, and then take the test at the end to see how you're doing.

Science

Science topics are both informative and fascinating. Learning about the amazing diversity of life forms on the planet is one of the most enjoyable parts of school for many students, and for some, biology becomes a life-long pursuit. The same is true about the study of our planet, our solar system, and the universe. Other areas of science are equally as engrossing. There are many difference facets of science, and all of them have an impact on our lives in a myriad of ways. You'll need to do well in this subject in order to earn your high school diploma. Here are some questions that can help you make sure you're on track when it comes to science.

1. How does the Sun compare to other stars in the galaxy?
    a. The Sun is much larger than most other stars in the galaxy.
    b. The Sun is much smaller than most other stars in the galaxy.
    c. The Sun is a typical star like many others in the galaxy.
    d. Technically, the Sun is not a star.

Directions: Use the information below and your knowledge of science to answer questions 2–3.

A student measured the mass and volume of blocks of different unknown materials and recorded his measurements in the following table. (Each block is made of a uniform material.)

Block:	Volume:	Mass:
A	10.2 cm^3	23.2 g
B	22.0 cm^3	30.0 g
C	35.5 cm^3	50.0 g
D	50.5 cm^3	75.9 g

2. Which block has the highest density?
    a. A
    b. B
    c. C
    d. D

3. Suppose that block C is split into two equal parts. How would you expect the density of each part to compare with the density of the original?
    a. Each half would have half the density of the original block.
    b. Each half would have the same density as the original block.
    c. Each half would have twice the density of the original block.
    d. There is not enough information given to answer the question.

4. What is the ultimate source of energy for most ecosystems on Earth?
    a. The chemical energy in soil
    b. The gravitational energy of the Earth
    c. The electromagnetic energy in sunlight
    d. The kinetic energy of the wind and currents

Directions: *Use the information below and your knowledge of science to answer questions 5–7.*

One burgeoning current field in space science is the search for exoplanets, planets orbiting stars other than our Sun. The following graph shows the mass of all exoplanets, with mass listed on the online exoplanet database. (M_J is the mass of Jupiter, so $1/10$ M_J means $1/10$ the mass of Jupiter.)

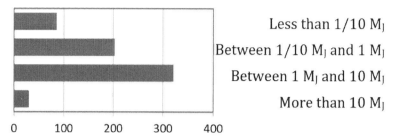

Less than $1/10$ M_J

Between $1/10$ M_J and 1 M_J

Between 1 M_J and 10 M_J

More than 10 M_J

5. About what percentage of these exoplanets have a larger mass than Jupiter?
  a. 15 percent
  b. 55 percent
  c. 85 percent
  d. 100 percent

6. Using current methods of finding extrasolar planets, larger (more-massive) extrasolar planets are much easier to detect than smaller ones. Given this fact, how would you expect the actual percentage of exoplanets that have a larger mass than Jupiter to compare with the percentage above?
  a. The actual percentage would be smaller.
  b. The actual percentage would be larger.
  c. The two percentages would be the same.
  d. All exoplanets should have a mass larger than Jupiter.

7. Given the definition of an exoplanet, which of the following would qualify as exoplanets?
  a. Mercury
  b. Saturn
  c. The Sun
  d. None of these

8. Yellowfin tuna prey on smaller fish and are preyed on by sharks. Which of the following is NOT likely to lead in the short term to a decrease in the yellowfin tuna population?
  a. A decrease in the shark population
  b. A decrease in the population of smaller fish
  c. Excessive fishing of yellowfin tuna
  d. Pollution of the tuna's habitat

9. Which of the following best describes the role the yellowfin tuna plays in the ecosystem?
  a. Producer
  b. Primary consumer
  c. Consumer, but not primary consumer
  d. Decomposer

Directions: *Use the information below and your knowledge of science to answer questions 10–12.*

A student heats water at different locations, measuring the temperature at which the water boils. He then plots a graph of this temperature versus the altitude of each location, as follows:

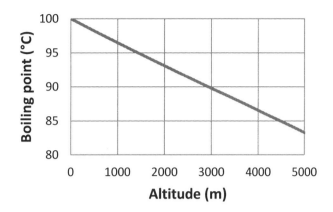

10. Which of the following does this graph best show?
    a. The dependency of boiling point upon altitude
    b. The dependency of altitude upon boiling point
    c. The fact that the boiling point of water is constant
    d. The fact that boiling point is proportional to altitude

11. According to the student's chart, what would be the approximate boiling point of water at an altitude of 3,000 meters?
    a. 85°
    b. 90°
    c. 95°
    d. 100°

12. Boiling is the change of state from a liquid to a gas. What is the term for the reverse process, the change from a gas to a liquid?
    a. Melting
    b. Freezing
    c. Sublimation
    d. Condensation

13. Sandstone is formed by the accumulation of sand grains that are compacted and cemented together by calcite and other minerals. What kind of rock is sandstone?
    a. Igneous
    b. Metamorphic
    c. Sedimentary
    d. None of these

14. What is one difference between sand and soil?
    a. Sand consists of only one kind of rock; soil consists of all three kinds.
    b. The upper layer of the ground is always covered in soil; sand makes up a lower layer.
    c. Unlike pure sand, soil contains water.
    d. Unlike pure sand, soil contains decomposed organic matter.

15. The water that flows beneath the Earth's surface, within soil or through cracks in rocks, is called:

    a. Groundwater
    b. The hydrosphere
    c. Runoff
    d. Spring water

16. What is the term for the study of animals?

    a. Biology
    b. Botany
    c. Herpetology
    d. Zoology

17. What is the term for a pure substance that cannot be broken down chemically?

    a. Compound
    b. Element
    c. Halogen
    d. Molecule

18. What is the outer layer of the Earth called?

    a. Core
    b. Lithosphere
    c. Mantle
    d. Stratosphere

Directions: *Use the information below and your knowledge of science to answer questions 19–20.*

A certain plant can have either red or yellow flowers. The flower color is controlled by a single gene, where the red color is dominant.

19. Suppose that a heterozygous red flower is crossed with a yellow flower. Which of the following Punnett squares accurately shows the possible results?

a.
	R	r
r	Rr	rr
r	Rr	rr

b.
	R	r
r	Rr	Rr
r	Rr	Rr

c.
	R	r
r	RR	Rr
r	Rr	rr

d.
	R	r
r	RR	Rr
r	RR	Rr

20. A botanist finds a different plant that also has red and yellow flowers and decides to breed them to find whether the red or yellow color is dominant. He breeds two red flowers and gets a mixture of red and yellow offspring. He breeds two yellow flowers and also gets a mixture of red and yellow offspring. Which of the following is the best explanation for this result?

    a. The red color is dominant in this species.
    b. The yellow color is dominant in this species.
    c. The color in this species is determined by more than one gene.
    d. This species of plant is capable of asexual reproduction.

21. Why is a glass window transparent?
    a. Light is absorbed by the window.
    b. Light is reflected by the window.
    c. Light is scattered by the window.
    d. Light is transmitted by the window.

22. When two chemicals react, what happens to their internal energy?
    a. The chemicals' energy remains constant.
    b. The chemicals absorb energy from their surroundings.
    c. The chemicals release energy into their surroundings.
    d. The chemicals may either absorb or release energy, depending on the reaction.

23. Fossils of marine organisms, such as trilobites and whales, are sometimes found in mountains. What is the best explanation for this fact?
    a. The oceans were much deeper in the past than they are today.
    b. Tectonic activity raised up land that was once part of an ocean floor.
    c. The organisms were carried from the oceans to mountains by predators.
    d. Despite their appearance, these organisms must really have lived on the land.

24. What force keeps the Earth in orbit around the Sun?
    a. Electricity
    b. Friction
    c. Gravity
    d. Heat

25. Which of the following can NOT be present in a single-celled organism?
    a. Cell walls
    b. Genes
    c. Proteins
    d. Tissues

26. A person with a bacterial infection notes that his urine has a strong, unpleasant smell. In which system is it MOST likely that the infection is present?
    a. Circulatory
    b. Excretory
    c. Nervous
    d. Respiratory

27. Joe pushes a block at a constant speed in a straight line across a cement floor. How does the force he exerts compare to the force of friction on the block?
    a. The force Joe exerts must be much larger than the force of friction on the block.
    b. The force Joe exerts must be much smaller than the force of friction on the block.
    c. The force Joe exerts is the same as the force of friction on the block but in the opposite direction.
    d. The force Joe exerts is the same as the force of friction on the block and in the same direction.

28. In Lima, Peru, an earthquake one day has a local magnitude of 3.5 on the Richter scale. Two weeks later, another earthquake has a local magnitude of 4.0. Which of the following MUST be true about the two earthquakes?

    a. The second earthquake was larger, and its epicenter was closer to Lima.
    b. The second earthquake was larger, but its epicenter was farther away.
    c. The second earthquake was smaller, but its epicenter was closer to Lima.
    d. Either the second earthquake was larger or its epicenter was closer to Lima, but not necessarily both.

29. If a cold-blooded animal such as a lizard senses that its body temperature is getting too low, which of the following is it MOST likely to do?

    a. Eat more to generate more internal energy
    b. Hide in the shade under a rock
    c. Position itself in an area of direct sunlight
    d. None of these

30. Organisms have some naturally occurring variations in their traits; variations that tend to aid an organism's survival tend to be passed on because organisms with those variations are more likely to survive and have offspring. Which of the following terms describes this process?

    a. Natural selection
    b. Artificial selection
    c. Mendelian genetics
    d. Inheritance of acquired characteristics

31. Why are coastal temperatures generally more constant and moderate than inland temperatures at the same latitude?

    a. The water of the ocean absorbs heat during the summer and releases it in winter.
    b. The salt dissolved in seawater absorbs heat during the summer and releases it in winter.
    c. The flat ocean surface allows a lot of wind to blow, which mixes the air currents and moderates the temperature.
    d. The water of the ocean reflects sunlight, redirecting it back toward the land.

32. What word describes the wearing away of rock and earth by wind and water currents?

    a. Convection
    b. Deposition
    c. Erosion
    d. Saturation

One measure often used to approximately judge whether a person might have a healthy weight is *body mass index*, which is calculated from a person's height and weight. The chart below shows what categories people of various heights and weights fall into according to their body mass index.

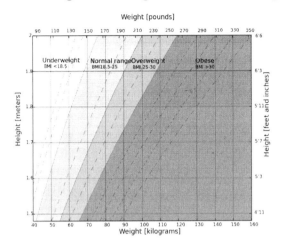

33. Ethan is 5' 7" tall and weighs 110 pounds. How would he be classified according to this chart?

 a. Underweight
 b. Normal
 c. Overweight
 d. Obese

34. Some animals, such as bears and ground squirrels, undergo long periods of inactivity during the winter during which they live off their stored fat. What is this process called?

 a. Estivation
 b. Hibernation
 c. Insomnia
 d. Somnambulism

Directions: Use the information below and your knowledge of science to answer questions 35–36.

A student decides to measure the electrical current through a small piece of plastic as she connects it to five batteries of different voltages. She graphs her data as follows:

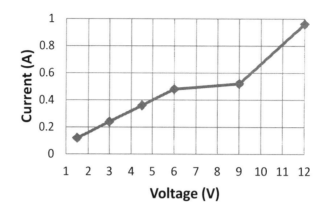

35. Which of the following best describes what her graph shows?
   a. Current decreases as voltage increases.
   b. Current increases as voltage increases.
   c. Current is independent of voltage.
   d. Current is equal to voltage.

36. The student made a mistake measuring the current for one of the batteries, but she doesn't remember which one. From the graph, which battery is the one with which she is MOST likely to have made the mistake?
   a. 1.5 V
   b. 3 V
   c. 6 V
   d. 9 V

37. High tides are slightly higher (and low tides are lower) around the time of the full or new moon. Which of the following is the best explanation for this?
   a. The moon is closest to the Earth at these times
   b. The moon is farthest from the Earth at these times
   c. The Earth is closest to the Sun at these times
   d. The Earth, moon, and Sun are all lined up at these times

38. Which of the following is the MOST narrow level of biological classification?
   a. Kingdom
   b. Order
   c. Phylum
   d. Species

39. If one sound has a higher frequency than another, how would you hear them differently?
   a. The sound with the higher frequency would have a higher pitch.
   b. The sound with the higher frequency would have a lower pitch.
   c. The sound with the higher frequency would sound louder.
   d. The sound with the higher frequency would sound quieter.

Social Studies

Imparting an understanding of humans and the societies and cultures they have created is the goal of social studies classes. This wide ranging field encompasses psychology, religion, economics, politics, anthropology, sociology, law, government, history, geography, and many other topics. No education is complete without a well-rounded course of studies in these areas. You'll find the following questions helpful as you seek to gain deeper insights into the world around you.

Civics/ Government

1. The first ten amendments to the Constitution are called the Bill of Rights. What rights are protected in these amendments?
   a. Environmental rights
   b. Governmental rights
   c. Corporate rights
   d. Individual rights

2. Which of the following best explains the idea of "separation of powers"?
   a. Powerful states must not be allowed to work together to dominate congressional votes
   b. Two or more political parties must always be in place so that no single party holds all power
   c. The United States of America's military should be split into branches of service that best facilitate their specialized roles
   d. Government roles are to be divided among several branches so that no single branch holds all power

3. Which of the following is NOT a branch of government?
   a. Executive
   b. Martial
   c. Legislative
   d. Judicial

4. Which of the following is a State Power?
   a. Maintaining a military
   b. Establishing a postal system
   c. Establishing schools
   d. Protecting patents

5. The illegality of falsely shouting "fire" into a crowd best exemplifies which of the following?
   a. There is a scope and limitation of rights granted by the Constitution
   b. Free speech is not a right granted by the Constitution
   c. Personal rights do not apply in public
   d. It is not illegal to falsely shout fire into crowd

6. Which of the following is NOT a requirement that must be met in order to become a citizen by naturalization?
   a. Show knowledge and basic understanding of United States' government and history
   b. Demonstrate appropriate fluency of the English language
   c. Live in the United States for at least five years prior to application
   d. Register for service in a branch of the United States military

7. The heads of federal departments who help the president make decisions are collectively known as what?

   a. Congress
   b. The Cabinet
   c. Secretaries
   d. A political party

8. There was much debate among the Founding Fathers over how to address the president. "His Highness" and "His Excellency" were both abandoned in favor of the title of "Mr. President." What does this title say about how the Founding Fathers viewed the role of government?

   a. The Founding Fathers wanted to establish of precedence that the government was on equal ground with the people
   b. The Founding Fathers were concerned that certain language would not be interchangeable in the event that a woman was elected to the office
   c. The Founding Fathers were prideful and expected the people to recognize their authority with reverence
   d. That Founding Fathers attacked the presidential title because they did not respect the presidential office or its authority

9. What is meant by the term "bicameral legislature?"

   a. A congressman who votes across party lines
   b. A three branch governing body that provides checks and balances
   c. A congressional body that meets for two sessions yearly
   d. A legislative body having two houses

10. The United States' government was originally formed under what?

   a. The Constitution
   b. The Bill of Rights
   c. The Declaration of Independence
   d. The Articles of Confederation

Geography

1. Which of the following most accurately defines the study of Geography?

   a. The study of people and the ways in which they are affected by, and affect the environment and places around them
   b. The study of land maps and how they describe specific places on Earth
   c. The study of Earth's physical attributes
   d. The study of the Earth's flora and fauna

Use this map to answer questions 2 – 3:

2. Using the map above, identify the region to which the state of Nebraska (NE) would belong.

   a. Northeast
   b. Southwest
   c. Northwest
   d. Midwest

3. Nebraska is southeast in relation to the state of Washington (WA). What is Nebraska's location in relation to the state of Ohio (OH)?

   a. Northeast
   b. West
   c. Northwest
   d. Southwest

4. Which of the following tools is the most reliable means of navigating today's oceans?

   a. An astrolabe
   b. A chronometer
   c. A Global Positioning System
   d. A sextant

5. What best represents a physical characteristic of place?

   a. Local customs
   b. Local wildlife
   c. Local monuments
   d. Local cuisine

6. Which of the following best defines "population density"?

    a. The average weight of a population
    b. The total number of people living in a defined area
    c. The total number of people living in a country
    d. The grouping of a population in a specific area

7. If you were to use latitude and longitude to classify a location, that location would be described as which of the following?

    a. Total location
    b. Relative location
    c. Super location
    d. Absolute location

8. What would best represent a human characteristic of place?

    a. Large bodies of water
    b. Governmental bodies
    c. Mountain ranges
    d. Regional climate

9. What is the best example of a physical geographic factor influencing American history in the 20th Century?

    a. The United States of America being protected by oceans from two world wars
    b. The United States of America's space program
    c. The United States of America's intervention in the spread of communism in Southeast Asia
    d. The Great Depression

History

1. What was the primary motivation in the rise of colonialism by European nations in the 17th and 18th centuries?

    a. The acquisition of natural resources
    b. The desire to spread democracy across the world
    c. Overpopulation in Europe at the time
    d. The need to prove that the world was not flat

2. The United States of America fought for liberty from which colonial power?

    a. Spain
    b. France
    c. England
    d. Mexico

3. The invention of the first reliable steam engine in 1775 marks the beginning of what revolution?

    a. The American Revolution
    b. The Steamboat Revolution
    c. The Digital Revolution
    d. The Industrial Revolution

4. The Americas were colonized by all but which country?

a. England
b. Spain
c. India
d. Portugal

5. Which explorer was determined to find "The Fountain of Youth" in the Americas?

a. Magellan
b. Ponce de Leon
c. Coronado
d. Columbus

6. Which of these states was not part of the original "13 Colonies"?

a. Pennsylvania
b. Rhode Island
c. Maine
d. North Carolina

7. All of the following countries fought on behalf of the United States during The Revolutionary War EXCEPT for which of the following?

a. France
b. Ireland
c. The Dutch Republic
d. Spain

8. Which of the following was the main factor in the United States' involvement in the Revolutionary War?

a. The country wanted no taxation from the British government without representation within their government
b. United States citizens demanded the right to bear arms
c. The United States did not want to offer quarter to British soldiers
d. The United States wanted the British government to stop interfering with their international trade laws

9. Migrant fur trappers, traders and settlers traversed The Oregon Trail through the Midwest to the West Coast from the mid-1830's until the late 1860's. Which of the following were hazards they encountered on their travels?

a. Hostile Native American tribes
b. Dehydration and starvation
c. Harsh weather conditions
d. All of the above

10. What approach did the United States initially take to World War I?

a. Nationalism: they celebrated their pride in the United States and felt that this made them united and strong
b. Militarism: they gathered an army and prepared to go to war
c. Neutralism: they did not want to be involved in international politics
d. Isolationism: they shut themselves off from interacting with other countries at all

11. What industrial change took place in the 1920's that allowed the cities of the United States to expand?

    a. The transcontinental railroad
    b. The first airplane
    c. The automobile
    d. Travel to Europe by steamship became possible

12. Which of the following factors prompted the United States to become involved in World War II?

    a. The sinking of the Lusitania
    b. The stock market crash
    c. The Nazi internment camps
    d. The Japanese attack on Pearl Harbor

Economics

1. This type of account is best suited for money that will be spent in the near future.

    a. Checking account
    b. Savings account
    c. Spending account
    d. Interest account

2. What tool is used to measure a nation's economic health?

    a. Gross Domestic Product (GDP)
    b. Totaling the number of trade partners
    c. The currency's relation to gold
    d. A survey of the population

3. Which of the following is NOT a perpetual resource?

    a. Energy powered by wind
    b. Energy powered by fossil fuel
    c. Tidal energy
    d. Solar energy

4. Which of the following best describes a natural trade barrier?

    a. War
    b. Tariffs
    c. A mountain range
    d. Embargos

5. The European Union does not have trade barriers between its member nations. What phrase best describes this policy?

    a. Trade incentive
    b. Free trade
    c. Liberal trade
    d. Laissez-faire Economics

6. What is another name for a plan on how to use the money you earn?

    a. A budget
    b. A balance sheet
    c. A ledger
    d. A financial statement

7. Which of the following refers to the personnel of an organization?

    a. Human Resources
    b. Human Relations
    c. Operational unit
    d. Consumer

8. What is profit?

    a. The total amount of money collected
    b. The success of a product in the marketplace
    c. The amount left over after all expenses
    d. A person advocating for a new belief

Vocabulary

Building a larger vocabulary is something you should plan to work at for the rest of your life. Of course, it's not really "work"; improving your vocabulary is something that should come naturally to you, and be enjoyable. Your vocabulary is simply the sum total of all the words whose meanings you understand. It may seem hard to believe, but by the time children are five years old, they already have a vocabulary that consists of well over twenty thousand words. Sixth graders usually know about fifty thousand words. That's quite a vocabulary! Now, this doesn't mean you actually use all those words on a regular basis. Most people use only a very small portion of their vocabulary. However, the more words you know, the more you'll have to choose from, and the better you'll be at communicating with other people. This exercise will help you expand the number of words you understand and use regularly.

For each sentence, choose the answer that is the closest in meaning to the word in italics.

1. Jogging trails were *abundant* in the area.

   a. rare
   b. plentiful
   c. dangerous at night
   d. extremely crowded

2. The boss's decision was very *abrupt*.

   a. sudden and surprising
   b. well thought out
   c. confusing
   d. long awaited

3. For good writing, it's important to *vary* one's sentence length.

   a. make the same
   b. make longer
   c. make shorter
   d. make different

4. Tom was very *lackadaisical* about his homework.

   a. excited
   b. thorough
   c. careless
   d. angry

5. I need a student with *legible* handwriting.

   a. readable
   b. cursive
   c. fancy
   d. slants to the left

6. His contributions were *meager*.

   a. just in time
   b. not necessary
   c. very small
   d. very large

7. In a *subsequent* lab test, the theory was proven wrong.

 a. expensive
 b. well known
 c. later
 d. scientific

8. The city council agreed to *diminish* tax abatements next year.

 a. expand
 b. reduce
 c. examine
 d. postpone

9. The babysitter said the kids were very *unruly*.

 a. tired
 b. well behaved
 c. poorly behaved
 d. ungrateful

10. Our first task will be to *replenish* the pantry.

 a. refill
 b. remodel
 c. repaint
 d. rearrange

11. I *loathe* operas.

 a. love
 b. hate
 c. don't understand
 d. regularly attend

12. Our efforts proved to be *futile*.

 a. harder than expected
 b. easier than expected
 c. very helpful
 d. useless

13. The conditions in that region are *arid*.

 a. very cold
 b. very rainy
 c. very dry
 d. very pleasant

14. A spirit of *cordiality* marked the negotiations.

 a. strife
 b. friendliness
 c. sadness
 d. happiness

15. Ted's a real *sleuth*!

   a. genius
   b. detective
   c. role model
   d. athlete

16. Mike is known for his *temerity*.

   a. being soft-spoken
   b. bashfulness
   c. boldness
   d. quickness to anger

17. Allow me to *paraphrase* what the governor said.

   a. express the same thing using different words
   b. express a spoken thought by drawing a picture
   c. give an exact quote
   d. explain

18. Robert will *mentor* the new employee.

   a. hire
   b. advise
   c. fire
   d. swear in

19. We read about Washington's *exploits* in class.

   a. personality traits
   b. wise sayings
   c. heroic actions
   d. ancestors

20. That was not *divulged* at the meeting.

   a. revealed
   b. explained
   c. voted on
   d. approved

21. The county commissioners voted to *abolish* the zoning ordinance.

   a. do away with
   b. strengthen
   c. support
   d. postpone

22. The sign's placement made the warning quite *conspicuous*.

   a. confusing
   b. easy to see
   c. hard to see
   d. unnecessary

23. The weatherman said we might experience a *deluge*.

   a. tornado
   b. severe snowstorm
   c. large amount of rain
   d. heat wave

24. Sally was surprised to learn about her cousin's *illicit* activities.

   a. previous
   b. having to do with writing
   c. charitable
   d. illegal

25. Participation will be *voluntary*.

   a. greatly appreciated
   b. not forced
   c. required of everyone
   d. done on a daily basis

26. I'm sure Principal Jones will *quash* these rumors.

   a. put a stop to
   b. find the source of
   c. punish someone for
   d. give an explanation of

27. Your dad sure seems *jovial* today.

   a. angry
   b. cheerful
   c. sad
   d. lonely

28. Some financial experts predict that the price of gold will *plummet* this year.

   a. go very low very fast
   b. go very high very fast
   c. stay the same
   d. go up and down repeatedly

29. His heavyweight champion title proved to be *ephemeral*.

   a. lasting for a very long time
   b. fraudulent
   c. financially rewarding
   d. lasting a very short time

30. First off, we must *perforate* the cardboard pieces.

   a. soak with water
   b. poke a hole in
   c. divide into groups
   d. hang on the wall

31. **Frank is the most *gullible* person I've ever known.**

    a. easily fooled
    b. good at swimming
    c. dependable
    d. friendly

32. **Well, the outcome was *astonishing*.**

    a. very enjoyable
    b. confusing
    c. predictable
    d. surprising

33. **If you do something every day, it can become *monotonous*.**

    a. a lot of fun
    b. easy
    c. interesting
    d. boring

34. **Sorry, but I'm not *omniscient*.**

    a. good at science
    b. good at math
    c. able to be in two places at once
    d. all-knowing

35. **This plant is a *hybrid*.**

    a. one that's a blend of two different kinds
    b. one that does well in warm climates
    c. one that was imported from another country
    d. one that blooms year after year

36. **I found him to be quite *insolent*.**

    a. phony
    b. rude
    c. intelligent
    d. helpful

37. **We have a *detached* garage.**

    a. unlocked
    b. two-car
    c. repainted
    d. separate

38. **I did my best to stay out of the *fray*.**

    a. fancy garden
    b. walkway
    c. fight
    d. fast-moving traffic

39. These old watches are very *elaborate*.

    a. containing lots of parts
    b. sturdy
    c. easy to break
    d. difficult to operate

Spelling

Being good at spelling is a really important skill for everyone to have, and that's why your teachers spend so much time on it. Being a good speller makes it easier to communicate with others, which is something you'll be doing all your life. It also makes reading much more enjoyable, because you won't have trouble recognizing words. Of course, you also need to be a good speller to do well in school. Good spelling is something you can develop with practice. This exercise will help you improve your spelling skills.

Spelling Exercise

Each question contains four words for you to consider. If one of them is misspelled, circle it. If they are all spelled correctly, circle NO MISTAKES.

1. appreceate	forty	inquire	poultry	NO MISTAKES
2. character	scarce	spagheti	verbal	NO MISTAKES
3. bachelor	violently	comercial	coarse	NO MISTAKES
4. saprano	temperature	glisten	destination	NO MISTAKES
5. barbecue	verious	negative	sequined	NO MISTAKES
6. infinite	asent	bauble	beautiful	NO MISTAKES
7. tuxedo	comfortable	wierd	chieftain	NO MISTAKES
8. plumbing	perforated	innocent	capeable	NO MISTAKES
9. patition	cooperation	prominent	advisor	NO MISTAKES
10. baratone	camouflage	autumn	paperweight	NO MISTAKES
11. pavilion	introduce	passenger	meteocre	NO MISTAKES
12. rural	nieghborhood	quiver	surgery	NO MISTAKES
13. emergency	hangar	naïve	nack	NO MISTAKES
14. improvement	frustrated	imune	feasible	NO MISTAKES
15. sailer	staggered	pastime	survey	NO MISTAKES
16. rapid	silluette	sculptor	niece	NO MISTAKES
17. prediction	bazaar	summersault	oblige	NO MISTAKES
18. bough	oyly	imitate	honorary	NO MISTAKES
19. resources	sensable	manila	vehicular	NO MISTAKES
20. choir	entertainment	lakker	debris	NO MISTAKES
21. denomination	omitted	advantedge	quartet	NO MISTAKES
22. eddition	interrupted	desecrate	bayonet	NO MISTAKES
23. horizen	gasoline	adequate	illustrate	NO MISTAKES
24. encouraging	suspicious	conscience	dewet	NO MISTAKES
25. familiar	enormous	testimony	racoon	NO MISTAKES
26. gazing	munopoly	proverb	manufacture	NO MISTAKES
27. vertical	obscure	crystal	beliddle	NO MISTAKES
28. scisors	jealous	creditor	colone	NO MISTAKES
29. governor	adjusted	apointment	apiece	NO MISTAKES
30. exploit	demonstrate	atterney	wholesale	NO MISTAKES
31. capacity	satisfactory	admirable	cafateria	NO MISTAKES
32. artificial	operater	aluminum	management	NO MISTAKES

Capitalization

One of the marks of being well educated is the proper use of capital letters. There are many reasons for using capital letters in written English. The main reason for capitalizing certain words is to show respect. Proper nouns, or names, are always written with the first letter capitalized. The same holds true for a person's title, when it is used as a form of address. Other titles, such as the titles of magazine, TV shows, books, plays, should also be capitalized. This rule also applies to companies, agencies, and institutions, as well as important legal documents and specific laws. In all of these cases, capitalization is used to show respect, or to set something apart from other things. Capitalization also makes it easier for readers to understand written English. That's why we capitalize the first word of a new sentence – to let the reader know that a new, separate thought has begun. In addition, if titles of books and movies weren't capitalized, sentences would often be very confusing.

This exercise will help you improve your capitalization skills. For each numbered item, read each sentence, and then decide if all of them are capitalized correctly, or if one is capitalized incorrectly. If one of the sentences is capitalized incorrectly, select the letter of the sentence which contains the mistake. If all of them are capitalized correctly, choose NO MISTAKES. Sentences may contain words that aren't capitalized that should be, words that are capitalized that shouldn't be, or both.

1.
   a. Next Saturday is Halloween.
   b. Did Reverend Johnson preach last Sunday?
   c. I can't wait for the super bowl!
   d. NO MISTAKES

2.
   a. Will you be going to College this fall, Joe?
   b. Did you hear that Emily got accepted to Barnard College?
   c. The Ohio State University Marching Band is the best college band in the world!
   d. NO MISTAKES

3.
   a. The bus will depart Lincoln Elementary at ten o'clock sharp.
   b. That Lincoln Continental belongs to Uncle Bob.
   c. I missed school because I attended Aunt Sally's Funeral.
   d. NO MISTAKES

4.
   a. We watched some TV Shows on Nickelodeon last night.
   b. Did you notice how bright Venus was last night?
   c. Clark Kent is a reporter for the Daily Planet.
   d. NO MISTAKES

5.
   a. Professor Goldberg teaches Principles of Accounting 301.
   b. Dr. Ramirez is Chairman of the department of psychology.
   c. My favorite course this semester is 19th Century French Literature.
   d. NO MISTAKES

6.

    a. I'm sorry, Sir, but we can't give you a refund for an item in this condition.

    b. We read about Sir Lancelot and his brave deeds in our English class today.

    c. Last night we watched To Sir, With Love on DVD.

    d. NO MISTAKES

7.

    a. What day of the week does the Fourth of July fall on?

    b. Last Winter was one of the mildest ones on record.

    c. Our town's 25TH annual Winter Wonderland Festival is next weekend.

    d. NO MISTAKES.

8.

    a. There are seven items on my shopping list.

    b. Can you name the Seven Wonders of the Ancient World?

    c. We will all meet right here at Seven P.M. tomorrow.

    d. NO MISTAKES

9.

    a. On our way to California, we flew right over the rocky mountains.

    b. The walking trails on the mountain were extremely rocky.

    c. We visited the Rock and Roll Hall of Fame in Cleveland.

    d. NO MISTAKES

10.

    a. Go ahead and laugh, but I really like Hamburger Helper.

    b. My little brother's favorite food is Mashed Potatoes.

    c. My sister loves Russian dressing on her salads.

    d. NO MISTAKES

11.

    a. In which month does daylight savings time begin?

    b. The first playoff game starts at 7 PM Central Standard Time.

    c. One of the biggest clocks in the world is London's Big Ben.

    d. NO MISTAKES

12.

    a. My parents used to watch the Brady Bunch on TV when they were kids.

    b. Our new Big Screen TV was delivered yesterday.

    c. I think Sanyo makes the best TV sets.

    d. NO MISTAKES

13.

    a. Charles Lindbergh made the first solo trans-Atlantic Flight.

    b. Today our class learned about the Battle of Bunker Hill.

    c. The battle took place in 1775, during the revolutionary war.

    d. NO MISTAKES

14.

a. What Breed of dog is that?
b. The Westminster Kennel Club Dog Show was first held in 1877.
c. It is held every year at Madison Square Garden in New York City.
d. NO MISTAKES

15.

a. Have you ever gone square dancing?
b. Dance marathons were popular in the 1930s.
c. The Twist was a Dance Sensation started by Chubby Checker in 1960.
d. NO MISTAKES

16.

a. I got an iPhone for Christmas.
b. My favorite thing about my phone is the Ringtones.
c. I like to play games on my phone, too.
d. NO MISTAKES

17.

a. Mom announced, "It's time for bed, kids."
b. "Please, Mom, can we stay up for another half hour?"
c. Then Mom said, "okay, but at 10:30 it's lights out."
d. NO MISTAKES

18.

a. My brother has to go to Summer School to make up classes he failed.
b. I started playing the guitar last summer.
c. The Hot Fun in the Summertime concert series starts next Saturday.
d. NO MISTAKE

19.

a. Who wrote As You Like It?
b. Did Alfred, Lord Tennyson write any Sonnets?
c. Do you want to get tickets for Shakespeare in the Park?
d. NO MISTAKES

20.

a. Please mark that date on your Calendar.
b. I think every office should have a wall calendar and a globe.
c. The Gregorian calendar is now used in most countries.
d. NO MISTAKES

21.

a. No matter where I live, I will always root for the Dodgers.
b. The Atlanta Braves used to be the Milwaukee Braves.
c. There should be fewer Quarterbacks in the NFL Hall of Fame.
d. NO MISTAKES

22.

    a. I never miss the rodeo when it comes to town.
    b. My aunt has been to the statue of liberty three times.
    c. Have you ever been to a three-ring circus?
    d. NO MISTAKES

23.

    a. Ladies and gentlemen, please welcome the President of the United States.
    b. Please rise for the singing of The Star-Spangled Banner
    c. Do you know the name of Canada's National Anthem?
    d. NO MISTAKES

24.

    a. I just love discovering a new Italian Restaurant.
    b. My mom makes much better lasagna than you can get at Olive Garden.
    c. Last week, Dad and Uncle Bob made their famous barbecue chicken on the grill.
    d. NO MISTAKES

25.

    a. Neil Armstrong was the first man to walk on the moon.
    b. Did anyone ever actually believe the moon is made of green cheese?
    c. There are only twelve Astronauts who have ever walked on the moon.
    d. NO MISTAKES

Punctuation

Punctuation is very important in written English. When sentences aren't punctuated correctly, readers get confused and messages get mixed up. You want to make sure you get your point across when you write something. To do that, you must use good punctuation. This exercise will test your punctuation skills.

The sentence in each question may contain a punctuation error. If there is an error, select the answer choice which contains the error. If there is no error, select NO MISTAKES.

1. Boise Idaho is the biggest city I've ever visited.

   a. Boise Idaho is
   b. the biggest city
   c. I've ever visited.
   d. NO MISTAKES

2. "Mom doesn't want us to have snacks before supper, Billy reminded Joanie.

   a. "Mom doesn't want us
   b. to have snacks before supper,
   c. Billy reminded Joanie.
   d. NO MISTAKES

3. Freida asked, "What time does the bus usually get here"

   a. Freida asked, "What
   b. time does the bus
   c. usually get here"
   d. NO MISTAKES

4. Sir, Pedro exclaimed, "you dropped your wallet."

   a. Sir, Pedro exclaimed,
   b. "you dropped
   c. your wallet."
   d. NO MISTAKES

5. The capital of France is Paris which has over 10 million residents.

   a. The capital of France
   b. is Paris which has over
   c. 10 million residents.
   d. NO MISTAKES

6. "Are those your sunglasses?" Molly asked?

   a. "Are those
   b. your sunglasses?"
   c. Molly asked?
   d. NO MISTAKES

7. "James and Kirk," said Mr. Brown "you need to see me after class."

    a. "James and Kirk,"

    b. said Mr. Brown "you need

    c. to see me after class."

    d. NO MISTAKES

8. Des, Moines is the biggest city in Iowa.

    a. Des, Moines is

    b. the biggest city

    c. in Iowa.

    d. NO MISTAKES

9. Dad said, "Lets go to the beach this Saturday."

    a. Dad said, "Lets go

    b. to the beach

    c. this Saturday."

    d. NO MISTAKES

10. "I don't think that's a very good idea Mabel," her mother replied.

    a. ."I don't think that's

    b. a very good idea Mabel,"

    c. her mother replied.

    d. NO MISTAKES

11. Does anyone know what time it is.

    a. Does anyone

    b. know what

    c. time it is.

    d. NO MISTAKES

12. Ms. Ramirez said "Class, it's time for a pop quiz."

    a. Ms. Ramirez said

    b. "Class, it's time for

    c. a pop quiz."

    d. NO MISTAKES

13. The bus should be here in just a few minutes?

    a. The bus should

    b. be here in just

    c. a few minutes?

    d. NO MISTAKES

14. "Mom," Janice asked, "when are Grandma and Grandpa going to get here."

    a. "Mom," Janice asked,

    b. "when are Grandma and

    c. Grandpa going to get here."

    d. NO MISTAKES

15. "I wouldn't do that if I were you", Dad said to Mike.

    a. "I wouldn't do that

    b. if I were you",

    c. Dad said to Mike.

    d. NO MISTAKES

16. The days of the week are, Sunday, Monday, Tuesday, Wednesday, Thursday, Friday, and Saturday.

    a. The days of the week are,

    b. Sunday, Monday, Tuesday, Wednesday,

    c. Thursday, Friday, and Saturday.

    d. NO MISTAKES

17. If you don't succeed the first time try again.

    a. If you don't

    b. succeed the first

    c. time try again.

    d. NO MISTAKES

18. "Stop this instant." the policeman exclaimed.

    a. "Stop this instant."

    b. the policeman

    c. exclaimed.

    d. NO MISTAKES

19. Mom said to Deepak "What did you say?"

    a. Mom said

    b. to Deepak

    c. "What did you say?"

    d. NO MISTAKES

20. I'm going you're going, Heather's going, and Eliza's going.

    a. I'm going you're going,

    b. Heather's going,

    c. and Eliza's going.

    d. NO MISTAKES

Practice Test Answers and Explanations

Reading

1. B: A simile compares one thing to another by using "like" or "as"; the only simile in paragraph 1—"like a mirage"—refers to the path.

2. C: "Landlocked" means "not on a waterway."

3. A: This information is found in Paragraph 5: "In March of 1973, the first Anchorage to Nome Iditarod Trail race was organized and held. This race was much longer than previous races, covering more than 1,000 miles—the whole Iditarod Trail."

4. D: This is an informational article – the author's main purpose in writing this article is to educate the reader about the Iditarod Trail.

5. D: The descriptive word "desperate" and the descriptive phrase "cry for help" are used in reference to the doctors in Nome in 1925.

6. A: Historical overviews, like this one, are best written in the third-person point of view.

7. C: We learn in Paragraph 5 that the Iditarod Trail became a National Historic Trail in 1978.

8. B: This answer offers the most accurate summary of the history of the Iditarod Trail race.

9. A: This article is organized chronologically, from earliest to latest dates.

10. C: is a supporting detail that expands on a main idea from the article. A, B, and D are not the best choices because they are all main points in the article instead of supporting details.

11. B: We learn in Paragraph 7 that the race participants receive their racing order numbers at the first mushers' banquet.

12. D: We learn in Paragraph 8 that, as they begin the Iditarod Trail race, mushers are separated by two-minute intervals.

13. C: The phrase "ancient history" is a figure of speech. Amy uses it to communicate that she has totally forgotten about the fight.

14. A: Scene 1 is set on the school steps.

15. C: Scene 2 and Scene 3 take place in a cosmetics store.

16. B: Scene 2 contains the climax of the play, when Jessica must decide whether to go along with Amy or not. In a story, the climax is the most exciting part of the story, when the action or tension builds to a zenith. This occurred when Jessica learned that Amy was planning on stealing the lipstick.

17. C: Scene 3 contains the denouement of the play, when Jessica returns to the store to do the right thing. This is also known as the resolution of the story.

18. A: The word "gonna" is used to show Amy's slang speech pattern.

19. D: The use of "ancient history" in paragraph 6 is a hyperbole, a major exaggeration.

20. B: The tone of this play is conversational.

21. B: The underlying theme of the play is that you should always do the right thing, even when it's difficult. This could also be called the moral of the story.

22. A: In Paragraph 21, Amy tries to justify stealing the tubes of lipstick by saying that the store has a lot of them, and stealing only two or three of them won't do any harm because they won't even be missed.

23. D: In Paragraph 18, Jessica says the lipstick is too "spendy" for her, meaning it's too expensive, and she adds that she's trying to save money.

24. C: is the most accurate and complete summary of the play.

25. B: "Forlornly" is best defined as "with a sad spirit."

26. A: most accurately represents the main theme of the story.

27. C: This story is written in the third person. That means the author is writing from the point of view of a narrator – someone who knows all the details of the story but isn't involved in it.

28. D: is only option that offers a supporting detail, while the rest of the answer choices represent important parts of the story.

29. B: In paragraph 8, Kaylee compliments Megan's singing to help her feel better.

30. A: If someone is "elated", they are extremely happy and excited about something.

31. D: The first sentence of paragraph 4 uses a simile when it says Scott "stood like a statue." A simile uses "like" or "as" to compare one thing to another.

32. B: most clearly and completely expresses the theme of the story. Coach Travis tells Scott that "it's all about perspective", and then says that how Scott decides to look at it is up to him.

33. C: is the most complete and accurate summary of the story overall. A, B, and D are incorrect because they cover only part of the story or some of the main ideas and concepts.

34. A: Scott is upset in the story because he feels responsible for the team's loss.

35. C: Scott and Megan are most similar in their feelings of disappointment in themselves.

36. D: clearly reflects a general theme found in both stories.

37. B: This story is set at a homeless shelter.

38. A: This story is written in the style of a memoir, as evidenced by the first-person, reflective tone.

39. C: offers the best definition of "stereotype" as it is used in paragraph 9.

40. A: This story is written in first person. That means the author is involved in the events of the story and is telling it from his point of view.

41. D: The main theme of the story is that homelessness is everybody's problem. One clue that this is the main point of the story is that the author clearly states it in the last line of the story. It's not always true that the last line of a short piece contains the main point, but that is often the case.

42. C: In paragraph 3 the author uses a simile to compare the size of the pile of potatoes to Mt. Everest.

43. B: Cranberry sauce was not served as part of the Thanksgiving dinner at the shelter.

44. D: The death of Chris's dad was the major problem the family had to deal with that eventually led to the their homelessness.

45. C: After meeting Chris, Ben had a completely different view of homelessness. Prior to the Thanksgiving meal, Ben thought homeless people were nothing but a bunch of old, filthy drunks and drug addicts. Meeting Ben and his family helped him understand that homelessness can happen to all kinds of people.

46. A: The author's intention in writing this piece is to persuade the reader to do something about homelessness.

47. B: is the most complete and accurate summary of the story.

48. D: is the best choice because the last paragraph of the story indicates that Ben is likely to serve at a homeless shelter again soon.

Written Expression

1. D: because this sentence is the simplest way to explain where Charlie was born. A is not correct because two sentences are not necessary. The additional subject and verb are unnecessary to express the idea. B is not correct, because *Near a small town and on a farm* is a fragment. C is not correct, because the sentences contain awkward wording. The sentences need to be combined in order to express the idea in the simplest form.

2. A: because in this sentence, *crops* has been misspelled as *corps*. B is not correct, because the subject of the sentence, *mornings*, is plural. Therefore, the verb also must be plural for correct subject verb agreement. C is not correct, because this sentence does not need a comma.

3. B: because irregardless is not a word. The correct word is *regardless.* A is not correct because *complains* is in the present tense, while the rest of the paragraph is in the past tense. C is not correct, because a comma is needed after an introductory clause.

4. C: because this sentence supports both sentence 10 and sentence 11. The sentence supports the cause and effect idea that the attack on Pearl Harbor prompted the United States to become involved in the war, which caused Charlie to enlist in the army. A is not correct. Although this sentence provides new information, it does not link and support sentences 10 and 11. B is not correct. Although this sentence provides new information, it does not link and support sentences 10 and 11. D is not correct. Although this sentence provides new information, it does not link and support sentences 10 and 11.

5. A: because *European* is a proper noun and must be capitalized. B is not correct, because *becomes* is in the present tense, and the rest of the paragraph is written in the past tense. C is not correct, because a comma is not needed after *champion.*

6. B: because this sentence uses commas in a series as it lists aspects of Charlie's life after the war. Both *returned to Kentucky* and *married a woman named Bethany* are events that have happened and therefore need to be separated by a comma. A is not correct. *Returns* is in the present tense, and the rest of the paragraph is written in the past tense. C is not correct. The correct sentence uses commas in a series, and therefore only uses one *and* in the sentence.

7. D: because the sentence is correct as written. A is not correct. Although the rest of the essay is written in the past tense, the last paragraph begins with *Today* and is written in the present tense. Therefore, *loves* is correct. B is not correct, because this sentence does not need a comma. C is not correct. Both *beside* and *besides* are prepositions, but *beside* means "next to" and *besides* means "in addition to" or "other than." *Beside* is used in this sentence as "next to."

8. C: because in this sentence, *through* has been misspelled as *though*. A is not correct, because *colors* is spelled correctly. B is not correct, because this sentence needs a comma after *strawberries,* since the sentence contains a list and uses commas in a series.

9. C: In this sentence, *sister's* is possessive and requires an apostrophe. A is not correct. *Flew* is the correct past tense of *fly*. B is not correct, because *week* is a noun and is spelled correctly.

10. A: because *realized* is misspelled in this sentence. B is not correct, because *street* is spelled correctly. C is not correct, because *look* is in the present tense, while the essay is written in past tense.

11. B: because a homonym has been misused. *There* is used to indicate a physical or abstract place, while *their* is used to indicate possession. A is not correct, because this sentence has two independent clauses joined by the conjunction *and*, and a comma is used before the conjunction. C is not correct, because *staircase* is one word.

12. C: because a homonym has been misused. *Four* is a number. A is not correct, because in this sentence *open* is used as a noun rather than a verb and does not need to be in the past tense. B is not correct. *Were* is plural, and *was* is singular. The subject of the sentence, *seats*, is plural; therefore, the verb also must be plural for correct subject verb agreement. D is not correct, because *hurried* is spelled correctly.

13. A: because this rewording of this sentence makes the meaning clear and is grammatically correct. B is not correct because this sentence is a fragment. C is not correct because the second sentence is a fragment. D is not correct because this sentence is a run-on sentence.

14. B: because a comma is needed before the closing quotation when the sentence is not completed with the quotation. A is not correct because *Oxford* is a proper noun and must be capitalized. C is not correct. The sentence does not end with the quotation; therefore, a comma, rather than a period, goes before the quotation mark.

15. D: because this sentence provides information that is not important to the rest of the essay. Answers A, B, and C are incorrect, because all of these sentences present content that is important to the essay.

16. D: In the previous sentence, the phrase *we continued to travel*, suggests a passage of time. A proper transition into the next sentence would involve the acknowledgement that time has passed. A is not correct because *however* is not a good transition into the sentence. B is not correct. Although *once in a while* relates to time, it does not transition well into the sentence given the context of the previous sentence. C is not correct. *Additionally* is not a good transition into the sentence because it does not indicate a passage of time.

17. D: because the sentence is correct as written. A is not correct, because a comma is needed before the closing quotation when the sentence is not completed with the quotation. B is not correct because this sentence does not need a comma. C is not correct because *says* is in the present tense, and the essay is written in the past tense.

18. D: because *motions* is in the present tense, and the rest of the essay is written in the past tense. B is not correct because *street* is not used in this sentence as a proper noun and does not need to be capitalized. C is not correct. A comma is unnecessary because the second sentence is not an independent clause.

19. C: because a quotation mark is needed to end dialogue. A is incorrect because *come* is in the present tense, and the essay is written in the past tense. B is not correct. *Too* means "also" or an indication of excess.

20. B: because this sentence is grammatically correct as written. A is not correct. The comma is misplaced and disrupts the sentence. C is not correct because the second sentence is a fragment. D is not correct because sentence 14 is a fragment.

21. A: because *their* indicates possession; *them* does not. *Computer screens* belong to the subject, *people.* B is not correct. *All around us* is an introductory clause and needs a comma. C is not correct. *Staring at them computer screens* is not an independent clause and therefore does not need a comma.

22. B: because the sentence provides additional information about the waiter. The sentence should be placed after the waiter has been introduced in sentence 20. A is not correct. The subject of the paragraph has shifted to the father at sentence 21, and therefore a sentence involving information about the waiter would be out of place after sentence 22. C is not correct. Sentence 18 provides setting information. A sentence involving information about the waiter before this sentence would be out of place. D is not correct. This sentence provides additional information about the waiter and should not conclude a paragraph.

23. C: because *waiter* has been misspelled. A is not correct. *Orders* is in the present tense, and the essay is written in the past tense. B is not correct because *himself* is the correct word, while *hisself* is not a word.

24. D: because the sentence is a statement, not a question. Therefore, the sentence needs to be punctuated with a period. A is not correct. In this sentence, *longhorn* refers to the mascot of a sports team and is a proper noun. Proper nouns need to be capitalized. B is not correct. *You* and *are* in this sentence are used as both a subject and a verb. *Your* indicates possession. C is not correct. *Football* is not a proper noun and does not require capitalization.

25. C: In this sentence, *batter's* is possessive and needs an apostrophe. A is not correct because *stared*, the past tense of the verb, *stare*, is spelled correctly. B is not correct. In this sentence, *dad* is not a proper noun, since it is not used as a name. *My* before *dad* indicates that it is not a proper noun.

26. B: because *saw* is the correct past tense of the verb, *see*. A is not correct because *blackened* is the correct adjective. C is not correct. A comma is needed to separate adjectives when each adjective separately describes the noun. D is not correct. *Into* is spelled correctly.

27. A: because *stares* is in the present tense, and the rest of the essay is in the past tense. *Stared* is the correct past tense of *stare*. B is not correct. *Me* is the object of the sentence because it is the recipient of the action, *stares*. I is traditionally used as a subject. C is not correct. *With hard eyes* is an introductory clause, and a comma is needed after the clause.

28. D: It is correct because the quotation marks after *out* indicate dialogue. Quotation marks are needed before *Shut* to begin the dialogue. A is not correct. When used as a noun, *everything* is one word. B is not correct. A comma is needed before the closing quotation when the sentence is not completed with the quotation. C is not correct. The sentence is not completed with the quotation, and therefore it needs a comma rather than a period before the closing quotation.

29. A: because this sentence is grammatically correct. B is not correct. When using the pronoun, *me*, in a series, it is always placed at the end of the series. C is not correct. The repetition of *and* is not grammatically correct. The nouns need to be separated using commas in a series.

30. B: It is correct because a homonym has been misused. *Hear* indicates the act of hearing and listening. *Here* indicates location. A is not correct. *Cheer* is in the present tense, and the rest of the essay is in the past tense. C is not correct. *Can* is in the present tense, and the rest of the essay is in the past tense.

31. B: It is correct because this sentence supports both sentence 22 and 23. The preceding sentence discusses noises coming back. The next logical sentence should have something to do with noises. A is not correct. Although this sentence provides new information, it does not link and support sentences 22 and 23. C is not correct. Although this sentence provides new information, it does not link and support sentences 22 and 23. D is not correct. Although this sentence provides new information, it does not link and support sentences 22 and 23.

32. C: because a proper transition into the next sentence would involve the acknowledgement that time has passed. A is not correct. *However* is not a good transition into this sentence since it does not require a shift in ideas. B is not correct. *Consequentially* is not a good transition into this sentence since it presents no cause and effect. D is not correct. *Therefore* is not a good transition into this sentence since it presents no cause and effect.

33. B: because *Imagine* is a proper noun. As the title of a song, it requires capitalization. A is not correct. *Favorite* is spelled correctly. C is not correct. *My favorite song* is not an introductory clause, so a comma is not needed.

34. C: The missing verb in this sentence must have something to do with possession since it discusses the band's success. *Had* indicates possession. A, B, and D are incorrect, because these verbs do not fit within the sentence.

35. D: It is correct because in the sentence, the article *an* is followed by a noun, *promoter*. *Promoter* begins with a consonant and a consonant sound and therefore must be followed by the article *a*. A is not correct. The verb in this sentence is *decided*, not *separate*, and therefore *separate* does not need to be in the past tense like the rest of the paragraph. B is not correct because the comma is unnecessary. C is not correct. *Solo* is not a proper noun and does not need to be capitalized.

36. A: because *Lennon's* is possessive in this sentence; therefore, it requires an apostrophe. B is not correct. In this sentence, *dream* is a noun rather than a verb, so it does not need to be in the past tense. C is not correct, because a comma is unnecessary.

37. A: because the sentence is missing the article *as*. This is the simplest way to express the idea of the sentence. B is incorrect because this sentence is not grammatically correct. C is incorrect because the first sentence is grammatically incorrect.

38. B: This is the simplest way to express the idea in a grammatically correct sentence. A is incorrect because a comma is missing after *song* and after *people*. H is incorrect because a comma is missing after *song*, and quotation marks are missing around the quotation, *"Imagine all the people."* J is not correct. A comma is missing after *song* and after *people*, and quotation marks are missing around the quotation, *"Imagine all the people."*

39. D: It is correct because the sentence is correct. A is not correct. This sentence is part of a longer quotation that began in the previous sentence. Since the quotation is continuing, the sentence does not begin with quotation marks. B is not correct. In a quotation, the punctuation is placed before the ending quotation marks. C is not correct. *You'll* is the correct contraction of *you will*.

40. C: In this sentence nice is an adjective rather than an adverb. It describes the noun, *sounds*, not the verb. A is not correct. *When I really listen to the words of this song* is an introductory clause, and a comma is needed after the clause. B is not correct. *Something* is one word when used as a noun. D is not correct. Although most of the essay is in the past tense, the final paragraph is in the present tense. *Realized* is in the past tense.

Mathematics

1. C: To answer this question correctly, convert all numbers to decimal form to make them easy to compare. Since two of the numbers are already in decimal form, we only need to convert $1\frac{7}{10}$ and $1\frac{3}{4}$ to decimal form.

$$7 \div 10 = 0.7, \text{ so } 1\frac{7}{10} = 1.7$$
$$\text{and } 3 \div 4 = 0.75, \text{ so } 1\frac{3}{4} = 1.75$$

Therefore, by comparing place values from left to right of 1.7, 1.72, 1.75 and 1.695, we see that 1.695 is least, 1.7 is next greatest, 1.72 is next, and 1.75 is greatest. So, Antonio should buy the border that is $1\frac{3}{4}$ inches wide.

2. B: To answer this question, one method that can be used is to convert all the fractions to decimal form so it is easier to compare them to each other. This can be done by simply dividing, since the fraction sign means division.

$$7 \div 8 = 0.875$$
$$3 \div 8 = 0.375$$
$$7 \div 5 = 1.4$$
$$4 \div 5 = 0.8$$

So, the only pair of numbers in which the fraction is equivalent to the decimal is in answer B.

3. D: Only answer D correctly shows each amount of salt being subtracted from the original total amount of 26 ounces that was in the box.

4. A: There is more than one way to solve this problem. One method is to use the fact that the number ends in 0. This means 10 is a factor. So, 10 × 75 = 750. The factor 10 has prime factors of 2 and 5. The factor 75 has factors of 3 and 25 and the 25 has two factors of 5. Putting the prime factors in order, least to greatest, and showing the three factors of 5 with an exponent of 3 gives us answer A: $2 \times 3 \times 5^3$.

5. B: To answer this question, that there are 9 equal-sized panes in the window. Of the 9 panes, 3 have a dark tint and can be represented by the fraction, $\frac{3}{9}$, which is equivalent to $\frac{1}{3}$. 2 of the panes are lightly tinted and can be represented by $\frac{2}{9}$. So, the number sentence, $\frac{1}{3} + \frac{2}{9} = \frac{5}{9}$ best represents the total section of the window which is tinted.

6. D: To find the difference, subtract. It is important to align decimal places. Note, when subtracting here, the digit in the hundredths place in 0.33 has no digit aligned above it. We must add a zero to 1.5 so that we can align the hundredths places correctly. Now we can subtract 33 hundredths from the 50 hundredths to get 17 hundredths. So, we get 1.17 as our correct answer.

7. A: Multiply 24 by 4 to get 96 and multiply 12 by 6 to get 72. Then, add 96 and 72 to get the correct answer, 168.

8. B: If each car brought from 1 to 3 people, then 50 is the best estimate of the number of people that could have arrived in the 25 cars. 25 is too low because this would mean only 1 person could have arrived in each car. 75 and 100 are too high, because then this would mean 3 or more people arrived in each car. The answer, 50 people, would mean that each car brought 2 people each, which is the average number of people who arrived per car.

9. C: To solve this formula, follow the order of operations. First, add what is in the parenthesis, 4 + 2, to get 6. Then, multiply the 6 by 35 to get 210. Last, we should add 20 + 210 + 47 to get 277.

10. D: Note that the ratio asked for is the number of people who ordered milk to the number who ordered juice. The number of people who ordered coffee does not matter here. This compares 10 to 25, and the order is important here. Since the ratio is with the number of people who ordered milk first, the 10 must come first. So, the ratio is 10 to 25, but the ratio can be written in simpler form by dividing both numbers in the ratio by 5, to get the ratio: 2 to 5.

11. A: One way to answer this question is to name the ratio: 200 to 240, then write the ratio in simplest terms by dividing both terms by the greatest common factor, 40, to get 5 to 6. It should be noted that the number of Grade 7 students is not important for this problem. Also, the order of the ratio matters. Since it asks for the ratio using the number of Grade 8 students first, the ratio is 200 to 240 and not the other way around.

12. D: To correctly write a percent as a decimal, the percent sign is dropped and the number is rewritten with the decimal point two places to the left. This is because a percent is always a value out of 100 and the second place after the decimal point is the hundredths place. So, 70% = 0.70 and the zero at the end after the decimal can be dropped.

13. D: There are 15 of the 20 assignments with check marks indicating a finished assignment. Since the fraction $\frac{1}{20}$ represents 5%, then 15 times 5% gives 75% of the assignments finished.

14. C: One way to find this answer is to set up a proportion: $\frac{6}{10} = \frac{G}{240}$, in which G represents the number of Grade 6 students living within two miles of the school. To solve the proportion, we should cross-multiply. So, 10 times G = 6 times 240. This gives the equation:

$10G$ = 1,440. To solve the equation we divide both sides of the equation by 10, which gives G = 144.

15. C: Looking at the chart, a pattern can be seen in the relationship between the number of gills and the number of fluid ounces. Each number of gills in the first column, when multiplied by 4, gives the number of fluid ounces in the second column. So, f equals 4 times g, or f = $4g$.

16. B: The formula for the area of trapezoids is not necessarily needed here to do this problem. Since the relationship between the area, A, and the height, h, can be seen in the chart, looking at the third and fourth columns to see if there is a pattern will show a relationship between the variables. Each value in the area column is equal to 6 times the value in the height column. So, we get $A = 6h$.

17. D: The amount charged for miles hauled will require us to multiply the number of miles by \$0.05. The charge for each load of \$80 is not changed by the number of miles hauled. That will be added to the amount charged for miles hauled. So, the equation needs to show 0.05 times miles plus 80, or $c = 0.05m + 80$.

18. B: To answer this question, start with the perimeter formula, $P = 2(l + w)$ and substitute values that are known to remain the same. So, $P = 2(l + w)$ becomes $P = 2(40 + w)$. Then we distribute, multiplying both numbers inside the parenthesis by 2 and get $P = 80 + 2w$. Writing the variable first in the expression gives us: $P = 2w + 80$.

19. C: An obtuse angle measures between 90 and 180 degrees and $\angle C$ is the only choice which measured in that range.

20. A: A right angle, by definition, measures 90 degrees and $\angle T$ is the only choice which has a measure of 90°.

21. D: The box symbol shown at $\angle R$ means that $\angle R$ measures 90°. Since we are told $m\angle S$ is 20° less than $m\angle R$, subtract 90 –20 to get 70. This means that $m\angle S$ = 70°. The sum of $m\angle R$ and $m\angle S$ is found by adding: 90 +70 = 160. The sum of all angles in a triangle always adds up to 180°, so subtracting 180 – 160 results in a difference of 20. So, $m\angle T$ is 20°.

22. B: The angles opposite each other in a parallelogram are equal in measure. So, $\angle R$ has an equal measure to $\angle T$, or 35°. The sum of the measures of these two angles is 35 + 35 = 70. The sum of the measures of all four angles of a quadrilateral is 360°. We subtract 360 – 70 to get 290. So, 290° is the sum of the measures of the other two equal angles, $\angle S$ and $\angle V$. Then we divide 290 by 2 to get 145. We know that $\angle V$ has a measure of 145°.

23. C: To find the diameter (distance across a circle at the center), the circumference (the distance around the outside of a circle) can be divided by π. However, since the worker put 2 strings of lights around the pond, and a circumference is just the perimeter going around the pond once, we must first divide by 2. So, 100 ÷ 2 gives us the circumference, which we then divide by π, giving the expression: $(100 \div 2) \div \pi$.

24. A: The distance across the center of the circle, 12 centimeters, is the diameter of the circle. The distance around the circle, drawn by Omar, is the circumference of that circle. The formula for finding the circumference of a circle is: $C = \pi d$. The expression that can be used substitutes the 12 for d and we get 12π.

25. A: Each of the units represents $\frac{1}{4}$ since there are 4 spaces between each unit. The point R is 9 units right of the y-axis, or $\frac{9}{4}$, which is equivalent to $2\frac{1}{4}$, and 14 units up from the x-axis, or $\frac{14}{4}$, which is equivalent to $3\frac{1}{2}$. An ordered pair always has the x-coordinate (how much to the right or left the point is) first, and then the y-coordinate (how much up or down the point is). This is why Answer B is incorrect. So, the correct answer is $\left(2\frac{1}{4}, 3\frac{1}{2}\right)$.

26. A: The distance from the top of the tire to the ground that is given is the diameter of the tire. The distance around the tire is the circumference. To find the circumference, multiply the diameter, 20, by π. Since 3 is fairly close to the value of π, 20 times 3 gives 60 inches.

27. C: A close estimate for the total time for all five runners is 125 seconds, which is found by adding 25.1 + 24.9 + 25.2 + 24.8 + 25.0. Then, to convert seconds to minutes, divide by 60 seconds (since there are 60 seconds in a minute) to get 2 with remainder of 5, or 2 minutes and 5 seconds.

28. C: The ruler is used to determine the length of one side of the triangle, which is about 4.5 centimeters. Since this is an equilateral triangle, all three sides are of equal length. To find the perimeter, we add up all of the sides. However, since they are all the same length, we can just multiply 4.5 centimeters by 3 to get 13.5 centimeters.

29. A: Since segment NM lies along the right side of the protractor, we read the inside scale. The segment NM passes between 60° and 70°, much closer to the 60°, so the correct answer is 61°.

30. B: There are 3 feet in every yard. Since we are converting from a larger unit to a smaller unit, we should multiply the number of the larger unit by the conversion factor. That is 120 times 3 equals 360.

31. B: There are 2 green sections on the spinner and the spinner has 6 sections in all. The probability of spinning green is 2 out of 6, when expressed as a fraction is $\frac{2}{6}$. Written in simplest terms, the fraction is $\frac{1}{3}$.

32. A: Only this tree diagram shows all possible color combinations of one dark color and one light color, where the two options of a light color are shown for each of the three possible dark color options. So, there will be six possibilities altogether.

33. D: The mean is just the average. To calculate this, find the total of all 10 numbers by adding. Then, divide that total by 10 because that is the number of data points. The total is 750, so the mean of this group of numbers is 75

34. B: Notice that the vertical scale should be 0 to 30 by 5's since each of the X's in the plot represent 5 students. Also, each column should represent a number from the line plot. For example, since Language and Sports Activities both show 5 X's, and each X represents 5 students, 5 times 5 = 25. The subjects of Math and Social Studies both show 4 X's, so 4 times 5 = 20. All of the values are found in this way and the only chart that shows these values is B.

35. A: The appropriate fractions can be found by putting the amount of money spent on each category over the total amount of money spent. $\frac{50}{120}$ is a little less than half, since half of 120 is 60. $\frac{30}{120}$ simplifies to $\frac{1}{4}$ and $\frac{40}{120}$ simplifies to $\frac{1}{3}$. This means that Sammy spent almost $\frac{1}{2}$ his money on shirts,

$\frac{1}{4}$ of his money on jeans, and $\frac{1}{3}$ of his money on school supplies. The graph in A best represents those fractions.

36. B: Since each person is paid by the number of miles driven, one must know not the total miles for the trip, but the miles each person drove. The fuel, weight, or hours do not matter for this problem.

37. B: To answer this question, find the total number of bulbs required by multiplying 10 by 3. The number of packages of bulbs required can be found by dividing this total number of bulbs, 30, by 5, to find that 6 packages are needed. Then, multiplying 6 by the cost per package, 8, we find that the total cost for all the bulbs needed was $48.

38. D: To answer this question, the total number of caps sold must be found by dividing the total sales, 3,360, by the price of each cap, 14. 3,360 ÷ 14 = 240, so 240 caps were sold in total. So, looking at the graph, it appears that about half of the caps were white, around 120. The graph also shows that the other 3 colors were sold in about equal numbers, so dividing the other half, 120, by 3, gives around 40. Then, adding 120 white caps and 40 pink caps, gives an answer of 160. The club had close to 160 combined sales of white and pink caps.

39. D: To find this answer, first estimate the distance the tip of the blade travels in one spin. To do this, we must first realize that the length of the blade is the radius of the circle. The distance the tip of the blade travels is the circumference of the circle. Using the formula, *C = 2πr*, we multiply the length of the blade by 2π (a reasonable estimate for π is about 3), so 2 times 100 times 3 is 600. This circumference is the distance traveled in one spin. Since the blade turns 15 times in one minute, we can multiply 600 by 15. We find that the tip of the blade travels about 9,000 feet in one minute.

40. D: This procedure first finds the area to be fertilized, by multiplying the length and width of the rectangular yard. Then, it divides that area by the area each pound of fertilizer will cover.

41. C: The first step would be to subtract the $10 he spent on the book from the gift, $40. This gives us $30. This is how much Tomas still has. We add the $35 he earned to the $30 remaining from the gift, which gives $65, the amount Tomas has in total. Then we subtract $65 from the $100 cost of the telescope to find the amount Tomas still needs to save.

42. C: Since the pattern repeats the same 4 figures, each multiple of 4 looks like Fig. 4 (4, 8, 12, ... , 28, 32, ...). The figure in the 31st position is one less than 32, so it should look like the figure left of Fig. 4. That figure is Fig. 3.

43. C: Notice that Set M starts with 1 and increases by adding 3 each time, so the numbers more than 20 in this set are: (22, 25, 28, 31, ...) Set V is the set of odd numbers, so the numbers in this set greater than 20 are: (21, 23, 25, 27, 29, ...) The first number common to both sets is 25.

44. D: Antoinette bought 2 pairs of earrings at $10 each. To find the amount of money spent on the earrings, 10 must be multiplied by 2. Then adding that $20 to the $12 she paid for the picture and also adding $7 for lunch, she spent $39 in all. $50 – $39 = $11.

45. B: It is easier to think as the required 16 inches as 16.00 and convert all answer choices to a decimal to compare. Anything greater than 16.00 would be sufficient. $15\frac{7}{10}$ is equal to 15.7, $\frac{47}{3}$ is equivalent to 15.67 and 15.5 remains 15.5. These three choices are all slightly less than the required 16.00 inches; therefore making 16.25 inches the only adequate choice.

46. C: Since she earns $5 for walking dogs and watering flowers, this term can be combined to simplify the equation. The other terms for bringing back trashcans and checking the mail are straight multiplication.

47. A: To correctly write a percent as a decimal, the percent sign is dropped and the number is rewritten with the decimal point two places to the left. If there is not two digits in the percent, a zero is used as a place holder. This is because a percent is always a value out of 100 and the second place after the decimal point is the hundredths place. So, 8% = 0.08.

48. D: Each of the units represents $\frac{1}{4}$. The point Z is 9 units right of the y-axis or $\frac{9}{4}$ units, which is equivalent to $2\frac{1}{4}$. The point R is also 9 units from the y-axis, or $\frac{9}{4}$, which is equivalent to $2\frac{1}{4}$. Be careful to notice that coordinate pairs always come in the order of the x-coordinate and then the y-coordinate, and is defined by the pair of numbers. The y-coordinate for Z is $\frac{7}{8}$, while Point R has a y-coordinate of $3\frac{1}{2}$.

49. D: To correctly order the numbers in this question, making the decimals all have the same number of digits by adding as many zeros as necessary to the numbers with fewer digits makes them easier to compare. Here, only 17.4 has fewer digits than the others, so add one zero to make it 17.40 (*this does not change the value*). Now, by comparing place values from left to right of 17.03, 17.4, 17.31, and 17.09, we see that 17.03 is the shortest, 17.09 is the next longest, 17.31 is the third longest, and 17.4 is the longest. Notice the question asked for shortest to longest, not longest to shortest.

50. A: In order to answer this question, we add the number of baseball and football cards to realize that there are 50 total cards in Castor's collection, 40 of which are baseball cards. To convert this to a decimal, we need to divide 40 by 50. This gives the correct answer, 0.8.

51. C: There is more than one way to solve this problem. One method is to use the fact that the number ends in 0. This means 10 is a factor. So, 10 × 63 = 630. 10 has prime factors of 2 and 5. 63 has factors of 7 and 9 and the 9 has two factors of 3. Putting the prime factors in order, least to greatest, and showing the two factors of 3 with an exponent of 2 gives us the answer: $2 \times 3^2 \times 5 \times 7$.

52. B: There is more than one way to solve this problem. One method is to find the least common multiple of 60 and 80. To do this, first find the prime factors of each number.

60 = 2 × 2 × 3 × 5

80 = 2 × 2 × 2 × 2 × 5

The factors common to 60 and 80 are 2, 2, and 5. The factors that are not common to both numbers are two factors of 2 from 80 and a factor of 3 from 60. To find the least common multiple, multiply all the factors without repetition. That is, multiply the common factors (2, 2, and 5) and the other factors (2, 2, and 3) together:

2 × 2 × 2 × 2 × 3 × 5 = 240

240 is the least common multiple. This is the total number of beads needed of each color. To find how many bags the club will need to purchase, divide this total by the number of beads that come in each bag for each color bead. 240 ÷ 60 = 4 (4 bags of blue). 240 ÷ 80 = 3 (3 bags of silver).

53. C: To answer this question, notice that this figure is a regular hexagon, having 6 equal sides and angles. The part painted darker can be represented by $\frac{1}{6}$. The part painted lighter is clearly $\frac{1}{2}$, which is equivalent to $\frac{3}{6}$. The whole figure is represented by the number 1. So, 1 minus $\frac{1}{6}$ minus $\frac{3}{6}$ equals $\frac{2}{6}$ which is equivalent to $\frac{1}{3}$. Therefore, the equation, $1 - \frac{1}{6} - \frac{1}{2} = \frac{1}{3}$ best models the part of the figure Olga left white.

54. D: To answer this question, note that the fractions have common denominators. When adding fractions with common denominators, we need to add only the numerators, so, the sum of $\frac{6}{10}$ and $\frac{8}{10}$ is $\frac{14}{10}$. This should then be written as a mixed number, $1\frac{4}{10}$, which is found by dividing 14 by 10 which gives the whole number and the remainder becomes your new numerator over the same denominator of 10. The fraction $\frac{4}{10}$ can also be written as $\frac{2}{5}$ by dividing numerator and denominator by the common factor of 2. Therefore, $\frac{14}{10}$ is equivalent to $1\frac{2}{5}$. Be careful here to remember the 1 from the original $1\frac{6}{10}$ amount given in the problem, which must be added to the $1\frac{2}{5}$ to make a total of $2\frac{2}{5}$.

55. C: First, multiply the cost of each tire, $144, by the number of tires, 8, to get $1,152. Then, divide 1,152 by the number of months, 18, to get the amount paid each month, $64.

56. B: 3,700 is the only answer between the minimum number of potatoes that could have been on the trailer, 150 X 23= 3,450, and the maximum number of potatoes that could have been on the trailer, 27 X 150 = 4,050. Another method that could be used to answer this question is to multiply 25, the number halfway between 23 and 27, by 150. The product, 3,750 is very near the correct answer.

57. B: To simplify this expression, use the order of operations. First, do what is in the parenthesis and subtract 1 from 3 to get 2. Then, we multiply 4 times 2 to get 8. Last, subtract the 8 from 40 to get 32.

58. A: The ratio asked for is the number of finches compared to the number of sparrows. This compares 16 to 20, but the ratio can be written in simpler form by dividing both numbers in the ratio by 4, to get the ratio of 4 to 5. It is important to notice the order of the ratio. Since the number of finches is written before the number of sparrows, the ratio must be 16 to 20 and not 20 to 16. Also, note that the number of wrens or jays does not matter here.

59. C: The ratio compares the number of coffee drinkers to the number of tea drinkers, in that order, so the ratio is 45 to 20. Note that the ratio of 20 to 45 would be incorrect. The ratio of 45 to 20 can then be written in simpler terms by dividing both terms by 5 to get 9 to 4. Notice that the number of hot chocolate drinkers is not important in this problem.

60. C: The 80% means 80 out of 100, which can be written as $\frac{80}{100}$. This fraction can be written in lowest terms by dividing both the numerator and denominator by the greatest common factor of 20, to get the fraction, $\frac{4}{5}$.

61. D: The number of shaded parts is 8 and the total number of parts is 10. This can be written as the ratio: $\frac{8}{10}$. Since percent is always a ratio with a denominator of 100, multiply both terms of the ratio by 10 to get the ratio: $\frac{80}{100}$, which can be written as 80%.

62. B: One method that can be used to answer this question is to write and solve the proportion: $\frac{3}{20} = \frac{V}{360}$, where V stands for the number of Brand V televisions that were sold at the furniture store. To solve the proportion, we can cross multiply: 20 times V and 3 times 360, which gives the equation: $20V = 1,080$. We solve this equation by dividing both sides of the equation by 20 to get $V = 54$.

63. C: Notice that there is a difference of 5 between the values in Column 2. This gives the "5" in front of n. Then, notice that if you multiply the position of the term by 5, the value is less than that product, by 4. So, the rule is $5n - 4$.

64. B: There is a one-time charge of $50 for the price of the phone and a $45 monthly charge in the first month for a total of $95. Then, a charge of $45 only is added for every month after that. Since the chart shows the total charge each month, adding $45 to the total due from the first month gives a total of $140 for the first 2 months. Then, $45 is added for the next month, for a total of $185 for the first 3 months, $230 for 4 months, $275 for 5 months, and $320 in total charges for the first 6 months.

65. D: The formula for the area of a triangle can be used here, but it is not necessary. To find the relationship between the heights and areas, look at the last two rows. A pattern can be seen that each value for the area, A, is just 15 times the value of the height, h. So, the formula is: $A = 15h$.

Science

1. C: The Sun is a main sequence star, a typical star about halfway through the stable part of its life cycle. There are many stars in the galaxy much larger than the Sun, but there are also many stars that are smaller.

2. A: Density is equal to mass over volume. We could calculate the mass over volume for each block, but that's not really necessary. By inspection, the mass of block A in grams is more than twice its density in cm^3 (23.2 is more than twice 10.2), while that's not true of any of the others. Block A is therefore the only one to have a density of more than 2 g/cm^3.

3. B: Density is a property of a material, irrespective of its shape. Because each block is made of a uniform material, no matter how the blocks are divided into pieces, the density of those pieces will be made of the same material as the original block and will have the same density. Looking at the problem another way, if the block is cut in half, each half will have half the mass of the original block, but it will also have half the volume, so the density, which is equal to mass over volume, will not be changed.

4. C: Most ecosystems on Earth get their energy ultimately from the Sun. Plants and photosynthetic microorganisms use sunlight to store energy through photosynthesis; primary consumers gain energy by eating the plants; and secondary consumers gain energy by eating other consumers. Soil comes from the breaking down of organic matter that was first formed due to these processes, so what chemical energy exists in soil is there ultimately because of solar energy. Living organisms do not generally get energy directly from the Earth's gravity or from the kinetic energy of wind and currents.

5. B: As a rough estimate, the graph shows about 90 planets with a mass less than 1/10 M_J, 200 with a mass between 1/10 M_J and 1 M_J, 320 planets with a mass between 1 M_J and 10 M_J, and about 30 with a mass more than 10 M_J. Adding all of these numbers, there are about 90 + 200 + 320 + 30 =

640 planets total. Of these, the number of planets with a mass larger than Jupiter is about 320 + 30 = 350. Proportionately, that's 350 / 640 = about 55 percent.

As an alternate, rough visual way of solving the problem, note that putting the top two bars together would make a bar just a little shorter than what you'd get putting the bottom two bars together. That means the bottom two bars (representing planets with a mass larger than Jupiter) are a little more than half the whole.

6. A: If larger exoplanets are easier to detect, then the observations of exoplanets are likely to be skewed toward larger exoplanets—that is to say, there is likely to be a larger percentage of large exoplanets among observed exoplanets than among the actual planetary population because there will be more small exoplanets that aren't observed.

7. D: *Exoplanets* are defined as planets that orbit stars other than our Sun. Mercury and Saturn both orbit our Sun, and the Sun is not a planet. Therefore, none of these meet the definition of an exoplanet.

8. A: If there are fewer smaller fish for the yellowfin tuna to eat, this lack of resources will tend to reduce their population and so will pollution (likely leading to greater disease and other problems among the tuna) and overfishing. Because sharks prey on the tuna, however, if there are fewer sharks, it's likely to result in an increase in the tuna population in the short term. (Of course, this isn't to say that decreasing the shark population is a good thing; sharks play an important role in the ecosystem, and a decrease in the shark population may have significant, negative, long-term effects.)

9. C: A producer is an organism that makes its own food, such as a plant. A decomposer is an organism that breaks down dead organisms. The tuna clearly doesn't fall into either of these categories. Nor is it a primary consumer, which is an organism that eats producers; the smaller fish that the tuna eats are not producers. The tuna would be a secondary consumer if the fish that it preys on ate plants and other producers, a tertiary consumer if the fish that it preys on were secondary consumers, and so on.

10. A: A graph is good for showing how a dependent variable (plotted on the y-axis) depends on an independent variable (plotted on the x-axis). In this case, the dependent variable is the boiling point, and the independent variable is the altitude, so the graph shows how the boiling point depends on altitude. Another way to look at it is this: The student is varying the altitude by going to different places and then seeing how that affects the boiling point, so he's seeing how the boiling point depends on the altitude. He's not somehow changing the boiling point directly and then measuring what altitude that puts him at!

11. B: To see what boiling point corresponds to an altitude of 3,000 meters, find 3,000 meters on the x-axis and then trace upward until the line intersects the graph. Then trace leftward to see where that falls on the y-axis. In this case, that ends up being a little less than 90°.

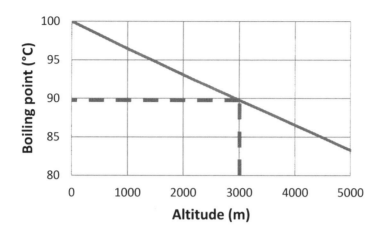

12. D: *Condensation* is a change of state from a gas to a liquid (such as when water forms on the outside of a cold glass, condensing from water vapor in the air). *Melting* is a change from a solid to a liquid, *freezing* is a change from a liquid to a solid, and *sublimation* is a change from a solid directly to a gas.

13. C: A rock formed by the accumulation of small mineral particles ground down from older rocks is a *sedimentary* rock. Based on the description of how sandstone is formed, it fits this description. (An *igneous* rock is one that cools from liquid magma or lava, and a *metamorphic* rock is a rock that was of a different type but was changed by high temperature or pressure.)

14. D: *Sand* is a collection of tiny particles of ground rocks and minerals. *Soil,* on the other hand, also contains decomposed organic matter. It is this decomposed organic matter that supplies important nutrients and allows plants to grow in soil and not generally in pure sand.

15. A: *Groundwater* is the water that flows through soil and rock beneath the Earth's surface. The *hydrosphere* is the term for all the water on Earth collectively, including the water in oceans and rivers. *Runoff* is water that flows over land. *Spring water* is water that comes from a spring, which by definition is above the surface of the Earth.

16. D: *Zoology* is the study of animals. *Biology* is the study of living things (not just animals but also plants, fungi, and microorganisms); *botany* is the study of plants; and herpetology is the study of reptiles and amphibians.

17. B: An *element* is a substance that cannot be broken down chemically and consists of only a single type of atom. A *compound* is a substance that consists of multiple types of atoms and can be broken down chemically. A *halogen* is a particular kind of element (halogens make up the second column from the right on the periodic table). A *molecule* comprises two or more atoms bound together, which may or may not be atoms of the same element.

18. B: The *core* is the layer at the center of Earth. Above the core is the *mantle*. Above the mantle is the *lithosphere*, the outer layer of the Earth (which includes the Earth's *crust*). The *stratosphere* is not a layer of the Earth at all but a layer of the atmosphere.

19. A: In a Punnett square, the row headings represent the genotype of one parent, and the column headings the genotype of the other. Each cell of a Punnett square should contain one copy of the gene from each parent, which means it should combine the letter from the top of the column it's in to the letter from the left end of the row. For instance, because the first column has an *R*, and the first row has an *r*, the upper left cell should contain *Rr*. Choice A is the only one that follows this pattern.

20. C: If the color of these flowers was determined by a single gene, then breeding two recessive plants would always show the recessive trait. In other words, if the red gene was dominant, then two yellow plants would always have yellow offspring, and if the yellow gene was dominant, then two red plants would always have red offspring. In this case, the trait doesn't follow Mendelian genetics, which most likely means the trait is determined by more than one gene. (It's possible that the plants can reproduce asexually, but it's irrelevant to the experiment.)

21. D: If an object absorbs light, the light stops at the object (a black object absorbs light of all visible wavelengths). If an object scatters light, the light bounces off the object (a white object scatters light of all visible wavelengths). *Reflection* is a special form of scattering where the light bounces off the object at the same angle (a mirror reflects light). If the light passes through an object, then the object transmits light—transparent objects, such as a glass window, transmit light.

22. D: Some chemical reactions involve the absorption of energy; others involve its release. A chemical reaction that releases energy is called *exothermic*; generally much of the energy is released as heat. A chemical energy that involves the absorption of energy is called *endothermic*.

23. B: The Earth's tectonic plates move around and often move under or press against each other, causing them to be raised up; this is in fact how mountains are generally formed. Over millions of years, this can result in land that was formerly part of the seafloor being lifted into a mountain. None of the other answer choices offer satisfactory explanations. Because fossils of land animals are also known from the periods in question (among other reasons), the oceans cannot have been deep enough to cover the mountains. It's very unlikely that any predator would seize prey in the ocean and then carry it all the way to a mountain. And while sometimes it may be hard to determine an animal's habitat from its fossils, if different kinds of marine organisms are consistently found in mountain locations, it's unlikely that scientists are mistaken about all of them.

24. C: The Earth continues to orbit the Sun because of the gravitational attraction between the two. Heat is a form of energy, not a force, and in any case has little to do with the Earth's orbit. Electricity (more technically electromagnetism) and friction are forces, but neither is responsible for the Earth's orbit; the Earth and the Sun are both overall mostly electrically neutral, so there is no significant electromagnetic force between them, and space is mostly empty, so there is no significant friction.

25. D: A *tissue* is by definition made up of groups of similar specialized cells, so a tissue cannot exist in a single-celled organism. Single-celled organisms do have genes and can have cell walls (i.e., bacteria do), and proteins are a basic molecular building block present in all known organisms, single-celled and otherwise.

26. B: The excretory system is responsible for producing urine from waste materials and includes organs such as the kidneys and bladder, which play a part in this process. If a bacterial infection affects a person's urine, the excretory system is most likely where the problem has its origin.

27. C: Because the block is moving at a constant speed in a straight line, there must be no net force acting on it. This means that the force Joe is exerting on the block and the force of friction on the block must cancel each other out. For this to be true, the force Joe is exerting on the block must be just as large as the force of friction on the block but in the opposite direction.

28. D: If an earthquake's epicenter is close, then the earthquake will be felt more strongly. Of course, a larger earthquake will also have a greater magnitude than a smaller one. Either one of these causes could account for the greater intensity of the second earthquake; they both don't have to be true. In fact, the second earthquake could be slightly farther away but much larger or slightly smaller but much closer. Therefore, Choices A, B, and C are all possible, but only D correctly describes what must be true.

29. C: Although cold-blooded organisms cannot internally regulate their body temperatures (which rules out Choice A), they can regulate them by external means (which rules out Choice D). If the lizard's body temperature is too cool, hiding under a rock (Choice B) wouldn't help; the lizard is most likely to put itself in direct sunlight to warm up (Choice C).

30. A: *Natural selection* is the term for the tendency of traits that give an organism a survival advantage to be passed on to its offspring. *Artificial selection* is the intentional breeding of organisms to get certain traits, as when humans breed dogs for certain desired characteristics. Mendelian genetics describe how some traits are inherited from an organism's parents but not why some variations are passed on more than others. *Inheritance of acquired characteristics* was the idea that organisms could pass on changes they acquire during their lifetimes; once thought by some to be the primary source of evolutionary change, it has now been mostly discredited, though it may occur in certain limited senses.

31. A: Water holds a lot of heat relative to most other substances; it takes a lot more heat energy to heat water than it does to heat the same mass of air or land. Therefore, in the summer in a coastal area, a lot of the heat energy goes into the water, leaving the land cooler. Conversely, in the winter, the ocean gradually radiates off the excess heat it absorbed during the summer, slightly warming the nearby areas. The salt has nothing to do with it and neither does the wind. While it's true of course that some light can reflect off water, it's not necessarily redirected toward the land, and even if it were, that wouldn't make the climate more moderate.

32. C: The wearing away of rock and earth by wind and water is *erosion*. *Convection* is a form of heat transfer by the motion of a liquid or gas. *Deposition* is the process of particles of solid being deposited on surfaces. *Saturation* refers to a chemical in a solution being at its maximum concentration.

33. A: Think of drawing a vertical line from 110 pounds and a horizontal line from 5' 7" and seeing where they intersect. They meet in the white portion of the graph, which is the part labeled *Underweight*.

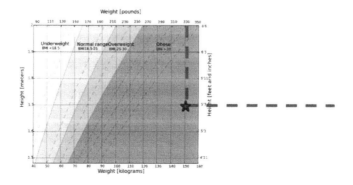

34. B: The state of inactivity that bears and some other animals go through in winter is known as *hibernation*. *Estivation* refers to a similar (lesser-known) process that some animals go through in the summer to avoid excessive heat. *Insomnia* means inability to sleep, while *somnambulism* means sleepwalking.

35. B: As you move to the right on the graph (corresponding to higher voltages), the y-value increases (corresponding to higher currents). So, the current increases as voltage increases. It is not, however, correct to say that the current is equal to the voltage—as a matter of fact, because current and voltage are measured in different units, saying they are equal to each other is meaningless.

36. D: To see which data point is most likely to be mistaken, look for the point that doesn't seem to fit the pattern of the others (an *outlier*). While it's certainly possible that this is a genuine data point that represents some unusual phenomenon, this is the one that's most likely to be in error. In this case, all but one of the points lie along a straight line, as shown below:

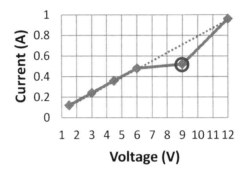

It's therefore the circled point—the point that does not lie on the line—that is most likely to be the one on that the student did incorrectly. Tracing down to the place on the x-axis this corresponds to, the chart shows that it corresponds to a voltage of 9 V.

37. D: The tides are caused primarily by the gravity of the moon; high tides occur directly under and opposite the moon due to the pull of the moon on the water. The Sun also exerts a pull on the water of the Earth, but because the Sun is so much farther away, the effect is smaller, and the moon's effect dominates. A new moon occurs when the Sun and the moon are on opposite sides of the Earth, and a full moon occurs when they're on the same side. In either case, the pull of the moon and the smaller pull of the Sun on the tides add together, leading to larger tides than when the Sun, moon, and Earth are not so aligned. (These especially large tides are known as *spring tides*.)

38. D: The species is the narrowest level of biological taxonomic classification of organisms. From broadest to narrowest, the most commonly used taxonomical levels are kingdom, phylum (for animals; division for plants), class, order, family, genus, and species.

39. A: The *pitch* of the sound—how high or low it sounds—depends on the frequency of the sound wave. The higher the frequency, the higher the pitch; a note pitched an octave higher has twice the frequency. The *volume* of a sound—how loud or quiet it sounds—depends not on the wave's frequency but its amplitude.

Social Studies

Civics/ Government

1. D: The first ten amendments protect individual rights. The Bill of Rights does not cover environmental or corporate rights at all; furthermore, these amendments only address the government's limitations of power.

2. D: Separation of powers refers to the principle of government being divided into three branches of power: executive, judicial, and legislative. The legislative branch issues laws, the judicial branch determines if those laws are constitutional, and the executive branch enacts and carries out those laws.

3. B: Martial law is not a branch of government. In the event that martial law, the military suspension of ordinary law, should come into effect, the executive branch would be in total control. Currently, the government is comprised of the executive, legislative and judicial branches.

4. C: The establishment of schools falls under the powers of the state. State governments do not directly oversee the maintenance of a military, the establishment or operation of the postal system, or the protection of patents. All but the establishment of schools falls under federal jurisdiction.

5. A: The rights granted by the Constitution have a scope and limitation. Committing an act with the intent to induce panic places other persons at risk and infringes upon their rights.

6. D: An immigrant need not register for military service in order to become a citizen of the United States of America. In order to become a citizen by naturalization, a person must demonstrate understanding of the United States' government and history, be appropriately fluent in the English language, and live in the United States for at least five years prior to applying for citizenship.

7. B: The heads of federal departments are collectively known as the Cabinet. The cabinet is made up of department secretaries, heads, and others whom the President deems necessary to the making of decisions.

8. A: The Founding Fathers wanted to establish of precedence that the government was on equal ground with the people. The Founding Fathers were not concerned with that a woman might be elected because women were not even permitted to vote at the time.

9. D: A bicameral legislature is a legislative body with two houses. The bicameral legislature was the result of the "Great Compromise," a deal between the Founding Fathers in order to level the playing field between small and large states.

10. D: The United States' government was originally formed under the Articles of Confederation. After the Articles of Confederation was deemed too weak to govern by, the founders came together to write the Constitution.

Geography

1. A: Geography is the study of people and the ways in which they are affected by, and affect the environment and places around them. The study of geography is primarily interested in how people relate to the world around themselves. Culture and ways of life are largely dependent on the environment that civilizations are situated in, it is for this reason that the study of geography is more than just the study and categorization of natural features.

2. D: Nebraska belongs to the Midwest region of the United States of America. Geographers break the world in to many distinct regions in order to make studying the world more manageable. Certain areas of the world share similarities that make it easier to categorize them as a *region* for the purpose of study and description.

3. B: Nebraska is west in relation to Ohio. Relative location is essential for understanding the world around us by helping to physically understand our location and the location of other places around us. From the question, we can gather than our starting point is the state of Ohio. From this point, we simply need to consult the legend in the bottom left-hand corner of the map to determine that Nebraska is west of our location.

4. C: A Global Positioning System is the most reliable means of navigating today's oceans. With the advent of new technology, specifically satellite technology, all other means of navigation has become antiquated. While these other means could still produce accurate results, they do not come close to producing the amount of reliability we find in global positioning technology.

5. B: Local wildlife best represents a physical characteristic of place. A physical characteristic can best be understood as a characteristic that is independent of human intervention. Cuisine, customs, and monuments are all manmade institutions.

6. B: The total number of people living in a defined area best defines "population density." Because population density is only concerned with a defined area, the measurement of a population's weight, the number in an unspecified area of a country, and the way a population is situated in an area are inconsequential.

7. D: Absolute location is classified by latitude and longitude. Latitude and longitude are points of measurement north or south of the equator and east or west of Greenwich, England, respectively. These points allow for precise navigation of the globe.

8. B: Governmental bodies best represent a human characteristic of place. A human characteristic of place is the converse to a physical characteristic of place. Human characteristics deal with elements of place that are intrinsically human.

9. A: The United States being protected by oceans from two world wars is the best example of a physical geographic factor influencing American history in the 20th century. The Great Depression, space program and intervention in Southeast Asia were not linked to physical geographic factors.

History

1. A: The acquisition of natural resources was the primary motivation for the rise in colonialism during the 17th and 18th centuries. Governments were constantly looking for resources in order to grow their influence. The promise of riches in the Americas, Africa, and Asia led European governments to pursue colonization.

2. C: The United States of America was a colony of and fought for liberty from England. Mexico would not found its government for many years after the United States' Revolutionary War and, while France and Spain did have a presence in North America, they did not govern the colonies that would become the United States of America.

3. D: The Industrial Revolution began with the invention of the steam engine in 1775.

The American Revolution would not begin until 1775 and the digital revolution would not come about for another 200 years. While the steam engine would be used with steamboats, there was no so-called "steamboat revolution".

4. C: The Americas were not colonized by India. In fact, India was itself a colony of England. England, alongside France, was responsible for most of the colonization of North America, while Spain and Portugal colonized South America.

5. B: Ponce de Leon is known for his search of the Fountain of Youth. The other explorers' goals, while ambitious, never centered on the quest for the Fountain of Youth. Columbus is known for his search to find a faster way to India, Magellan is remembered for being the first explorer to map a route from the Atlantic Ocean into the Pacific Ocean, and Coronado is known for his quest to find famed cities of gold.

6. C: Maine was not one of the original 13 colonies. The original 13 colonies are: New Hampshire, Massachusetts, Rhode Island, Connecticut, New York, New Jersey, Pennsylvania, Delaware, Maryland, Virginia, North Carolina, South Carolina, and Georgia.

7. B: Ireland did not fight on behalf of the United States of America during the Revolutionary War because Ireland was not a sovereign state until its own rebellion in the early 20th century.

8. A: Taxation without representation was the main factor that led the colonies to revolt against England. While the right to bear arms and the right to refuse quarter were addressed in later legislation, the catalyst to war was this taxation that the colonists felt was unfair.

9. D: Migrant fur trappers faced a host of challenges in the mid to late 19th century, including hostile native tribes, dehydration and starvation, and harsh weather. All of the above is the correct answer.

10. C: Initially, the United States maintained a neutral approach to the First World War. The government felt that what was going on in Europe was not the United States' problem. It was not until after the First World War that the United States would adopt an isolationist approach.

11. C: The mass production of Ford's Model T allowed cities across the United States to expand at an unprecedented pace. Steamship and railroad travel had already been well established by the 1920's and it would be several decades before air travel would be feasible on a large scale.

12. D: The attack on Pearl Harbor by the Imperial Navy of Japan was the primary factor leading to the United States joining of the Allies during the Second World War. The sinking of the Lusitania influenced the United States' entry into the First World War. The extent of the horror of Nazi internment camps was not fully grasped until the end of World War II. Finally, a market crash was not an influential factor in the decision to enter the Second World War.

Economics

1. A: A checking account is best suited for holding money that is to be spent in the near future; it generally does not accrue interest. A savings account would be utilized when the account holder wishes to not spend funds for the foreseeable future.

2. A: A Gross Domestic Product is used to measure a nation's economic health. Most nations no longer base their currency on gold, the number of trade partners a nation has is not indicative of their economic health, and while the general population's thoughts about the economy may be important, they are not necessarily valid.

3. B: Fossil fuels are not a perpetual resource; this energy source is formed by the decomposition of buried dead organisms. There is a finite amount of fossil fuels in the earth, while wind, the sun, and tides are a constant source of energy.

4. C: A mountain is an example of a natural trade barrier. Because tariffs, embargos, and war are all caused by and attributed to humans, they cannot be considered "natural trade barriers."

5. B: The European Union's lack of trade barriers between member states is an example of free trade. This was a very deliberate decision by the European Union in direct contrast to laissez-faire, or hands off, economics, which would not try to influence the market.

6. A: A budget is a plan for how to use income. A budget is a measure taken before trade has taken place, whereas balance sheets, ledgers, and financial statements are all reports of trade that has already taken place.

7. A: Human resources refer to the personnel of an organization. This is due to organizations viewing their employees as integral aspects of their product. The term human relations refers to the companies contact with their consumers.

8. C: Profit is the amount left over after all expenses. In other words, profit is the total amount of money collected minus the cost it took to produce the good or service. Profit is more than the success of a product, or the total amount of money collected.

Vocabulary

1. B: plentiful

2. A: sudden and surprising

3. D: make different

4. C: careless

5. A: readable

6. C: very small

7. C: later

8. B: reduce

9. C: poorly behaved

10. A: refill

11. B: hate

12. D: useless

13. C: very dry

14. B: friendliness

15. B: detective

Copyright © Mometrix Media. You have been licensed one copy of this document for personal use only. Any other reproduction or redistribution is strictly prohibited. All rights reserved.

16. **C:** boldness

17. **A:** express the same thing using different words

18. **B:** advise

19. **C:** heroic actions

20. **A:** revealed

21. **A:** do away with

22. **B:** easy to see

23. **C:** large amount of rain

24. **D:** illegal

25. **B:** not forced

26. **A:** put a stop to

27. **B:** cheerful

28. **A:** go very low very fast

29. **D:** lasting a very short time

30. **B:** poke a hole in

31. **A:** easily fooled

32. **D:** surprising

33. **D:** boring

34. **D:** all-knowing

35. **A:** one that's a blend of two different kinds

36. **B:** rude

37. **D:** separate

38. **C:** fight

39. **A:** containing lots of parts

Spelling

1. appreceate – this should be appreciate

2. spagheti – this should be spaghetti

3. comercial – this should be commercial

4. saprano – this should be soprano

5. verious – this should be various

6. asent – this should be assent (or ascent)

7. *wierd* – this should be *weird*

8. capeable – this should be capable

9. patition – this should be petition

10. baratone – this should be baritone

11. meteocre – this should be mediocre

12. nieghborhood – this should be neighborhood

13. *nack* – this should be *knack*

14. *imune* – this should be *immune*

15. *sailer* – this should be *sailor*

16. silluette – this should be silhouette

17. summersault – this should be somersault

18. *oyly* – this should be *oily*

19. sensable – this should be sensible

20. *lakker* – this should be *lacquer*

21. advantedge – this should be advantage

22. eddition – this should be edition

23. *horizen* – this should be *horizon*

24. *dewet* – this should be *duet*

25. *racoon* – this should be *raccoon*

26. munopoly – this should be monopoly

27. beliddle – this should be belittle

28. scisors – this should be scissors

29. apointment – this should be appointment

30. atterney – this should be attorney

31. cafateria – this should be cafeteria

32. operater – this should be operator

Capitalization

1. C: I can't wait for the super bowl!

Correct: I can't wait for the Super Bowl!

2. A: Will you be going to College this fall, Joe?

Correct: Will you be going to college this fall, Joe?

3. C: I missed school because I attended Aunt Sally's Funeral.

Correct: I missed school because I attended Aunt Sally's funeral.

4. A: We watched some TV Shows on Nickelodeon last night.

Correct: We watched some TV shows on Nickelodeon last night.

5. B: Dr. Ramirez is Chairman of the department of psychology.

Correct: Dr. Ramirez is Chairman of the Department of Psychology.

6. A: I'm sorry, Sir, but we can't give you a refund for an item in this condition.

Correct: I'm sorry, sir, but we can't give you a refund for an item in this condition.

7. B: Last Winter was one of the mildest ones on record.

Correct: Last winter was one of the mildest ones on record.

8. C: We will all meet right here at Seven P.M. tomorrow.

Correct: We will all meet right here at seven P.M. tomorrow.

9. A: On our way to California, we flew right over the rocky mountains.

Correct: On our way to California, we flew right over the Rocky Mountains.

10. B: My little brother's favorite food is Mashed Potatoes.

Correct: My little brother's favorite food is mashed potatoes.

11. A: In which month does daylight savings time begin?

Correct: In which month does Daylight Savings Time begin?

12. B: Our new Big Screen TV was delivered yesterday.

Correct: Our new big screen TV was delivered yesterday.

13. C: The battle took place in 1775, during the revolutionary war.

Correct: The battle took place in 1775, during the Revolutionary War.

14. A: What Breed of dog is that?

Correct: What breed of dog is that?

15. C: The Twist was a Dance Sensation started by Chubby Checker in 1960.

Correct: The Twist was a dance sensation started by Chubby Checker in 1960.

16. B: My favorite thing about my phone is the Ringtones.

Correct: My favorite thing about my phone is the ringtones.

17. C: Then Mom said, "okay, but at 10:30 it's lights out."

Correct: Then Mom said, "Okay, but at 10:30 it's lights out."

18. A: My brother has to go to Summer School to make up classes he failed.

Correct: My brother has to go to summer school to make up classes he failed.

19. B: Did Alfred, Lord Tennyson write any Sonnets?

Correct: Did Alfred, Lord Tennyson write any sonnets?

20. A: Please mark that date on your Calendar.

Correct: Please mark that date on your calendar.

21. C: There should be fewer Quarterbacks in the NFL Hall of Fame.

Correct: There should be fewer quarterbacks in the NFL Hall of Fame.

22. B: My aunt has been to the statue of liberty three times.

Correct: My aunt has been to the Statue of Liberty three times.

23. C: Do you know the name of Canada's National Anthem?

Correct: Do you know the name of Canada's national anthem?

24. A: I just love discovering a new Italian Restaurant.

Correct: I just love discovering a new Italian restaurant.

25. C: There are only twelve Astronauts who have ever walked on the moon.

Correct: There are only twelve astronauts who have ever walked on the moon.

Punctuation

1. A: Boise Idaho is should be Boise, Idaho is

2. B: to have snacks before supper, should be to have snacks before supper,"

3. C: usually get here" should be usually get here?"

4. A: Sir, Pedro exclaimed, should be "Sir," Pedro exclaimed,

5. B: is Paris which has over should be is Paris, which has over

6. C: Molly asked? should be Molly asked.

7. B: said Mr. Brown "you need should be said Mr. Brown, "you need

8. A: Des, Moines is should be Des Moines is

9. A: Dad said, "Lets go should be Dad said, "Let's go

10. D: NO MISTAKES

11. C: time it is. should be time it is?

12. A: Ms. Ramirez said should be Ms. Ramirez said,

13. C: a few minutes? should be a few minutes.

14. C: Grandpa going to get here." should be Grandpa going to get here?"

15. B: if I were you", should be if I were you,"

16. A: The days of the week are, should be The days of the week are

17. C: time try again. should be time, try again.

18. A: "Stop this instant." should be "Stop this instant!"

19. B: to Deepak should be to Deepak,

20. C: I'm going you're going, should be I'm going, you're going,

How to Overcome Test Anxiety

Just the thought of taking a test is enough to make most people a little nervous. A test is an important event that can have a long-term impact on your future, so it's important to take it seriously and it's natural to feel anxious about performing well. But just because anxiety is normal, that doesn't mean that it's helpful in test taking, or that you should simply accept it as part of your life. Anxiety can have a variety of effects. These effects can be mild, like making you feel slightly nervous, or severe, like blocking your ability to focus or remember even a simple detail.

If you experience test anxiety—whether severe or mild—it's important to know how to beat it. To discover this, first you need to understand what causes test anxiety.

Causes of Test Anxiety

While we often think of anxiety as an uncontrollable emotional state, it can actually be caused by simple, practical things. One of the most common causes of test anxiety is that a person does not feel adequately prepared for their test. This feeling can be the result of many different issues such as poor study habits or lack of organization, but the most common culprit is time management. Starting to study too late, failing to organize your study time to cover all of the material, or being distracted while you study will mean that you're not well prepared for the test. This may lead to cramming the night before, which will cause you to be physically and mentally exhausted for the test. Poor time management also contributes to feelings of stress, fear, and hopelessness as you realize you are not well prepared but don't know what to do about it.

Other times, test anxiety is not related to your preparation for the test but comes from unresolved fear. This may be a past failure on a test, or poor performance on tests in general. It may come from comparing yourself to others who seem to be performing better or from the stress of living up to expectations. Anxiety may be driven by fears of the future—how failure on this test would affect your educational and career goals. These fears are often completely irrational, but they can still negatively impact your test performance.

> **Review Video: 3 Reasons You Have Test Anxiety**
> Visit mometrix.com/academy and enter code: 428468

Elements of Test Anxiety

As mentioned earlier, test anxiety is considered to be an emotional state, but it has physical and mental components as well. Sometimes you may not even realize that you are suffering from test anxiety until you notice the physical symptoms. These can include trembling hands, rapid heartbeat, sweating, nausea, and tense muscles. Extreme anxiety may lead to fainting or vomiting. Obviously, any of these symptoms can have a negative impact on testing. It is important to recognize them as soon as they begin to occur so that you can address the problem before it damages your performance.

> **Review Video: 3 Ways to Tell You Have Test Anxiety**
> Visit mometrix.com/academy and enter code: 927847

The mental components of test anxiety include trouble focusing and inability to remember learned information. During a test, your mind is on high alert, which can help you recall information and stay focused for an extended period of time. However, anxiety interferes with your mind's natural processes, causing you to blank out, even on the questions you know well. The strain of testing during anxiety makes it difficult to stay focused, especially on a test that may take several hours. Extreme anxiety can take a huge mental toll, making it difficult not only to recall test information but even to understand the test questions or pull your thoughts together.

> **Review Video: How Test Anxiety Affects Memory**
> Visit mometrix.com/academy and enter code: 609003

Effects of Test Anxiety

Test anxiety is like a disease—if left untreated, it will get progressively worse. Anxiety leads to poor performance, and this reinforces the feelings of fear and failure, which in turn lead to poor performances on subsequent tests. It can grow from a mild nervousness to a crippling condition. If allowed to progress, test anxiety can have a big impact on your schooling, and consequently on your future.

Test anxiety can spread to other parts of your life. Anxiety on tests can become anxiety in any stressful situation, and blanking on a test can turn into panicking in a job situation. But fortunately, you don't have to let anxiety rule your testing and determine your grades. There are a number of relatively simple steps you can take to move past anxiety and function normally on a test and in the rest of life.

> **Review Video: How Test Anxiety Impacts Your Grades**
> Visit mometrix.com/academy and enter code: 939819

Physical Steps for Beating Test Anxiety

While test anxiety is a serious problem, the good news is that it can be overcome. It doesn't have to control your ability to think and remember information. While it may take time, you can begin taking steps today to beat anxiety.

Just as your first hint that you may be struggling with anxiety comes from the physical symptoms, the first step to treating it is also physical. Rest is crucial for having a clear, strong mind. If you are tired, it is much easier to give in to anxiety. But if you establish good sleep habits, your body and mind will be ready to perform optimally, without the strain of exhaustion. Additionally, sleeping well helps you to retain information better, so you're more likely to recall the answers when you see the test questions.

Getting good sleep means more than going to bed on time. It's important to allow your brain time to relax. Take study breaks from time to time so it doesn't get overworked, and don't study right before bed. Take time to rest your mind before trying to rest your body, or you may find it difficult to fall asleep.

> **Review Video: The Importance of Sleep for Your Brain**
> Visit mometrix.com/academy and enter code: 319338

Along with sleep, other aspects of physical health are important in preparing for a test. Good nutrition is vital for good brain function. Sugary foods and drinks may give a burst of energy but this burst is followed by a crash, both physically and emotionally. Instead, fuel your body with protein and vitamin-rich foods.

Also, drink plenty of water. Dehydration can lead to headaches and exhaustion, especially if your brain is already under stress from the rigors of the test. Particularly if your test is a long one, drink water during the breaks. And if possible, take an energy-boosting snack to eat between sections.

> **Review Video: How Diet Can Affect your Mood**
> Visit mometrix.com/academy and enter code: 624317

Along with sleep and diet, a third important part of physical health is exercise. Maintaining a steady workout schedule is helpful, but even taking 5-minute study breaks to walk can help get your blood pumping faster and clear your head. Exercise also releases endorphins, which contribute to a positive feeling and can help combat test anxiety.

When you nurture your physical health, you are also contributing to your mental health. If your body is healthy, your mind is much more likely to be healthy as well. So take time to rest, nourish your body with healthy food and water, and get moving as much as possible. Taking these physical steps will make you stronger and more able to take the mental steps necessary to overcome test anxiety.

Mental Steps for Beating Test Anxiety

Working on the mental side of test anxiety can be more challenging, but as with the physical side, there are clear steps you can take to overcome it. As mentioned earlier, test anxiety often stems from lack of preparation, so the obvious solution is to prepare for the test. Effective studying may be the most important weapon you have for beating test anxiety, but you can and should employ several other mental tools to combat fear.

First, boost your confidence by reminding yourself of past success—tests or projects that you aced. If you're putting as much effort into preparing for this test as you did for those, there's no reason you should expect to fail here. Work hard to prepare; then trust your preparation.

Second, surround yourself with encouraging people. It can be helpful to find a study group, but be sure that the people you're around will encourage a positive attitude. If you spend time with others who are anxious or cynical, this will only contribute to your own anxiety. Look for others who are motivated to study hard from a desire to succeed, not from a fear of failure.

Third, reward yourself. A test is physically and mentally tiring, even without anxiety, and it can be helpful to have something to look forward to. Plan an activity following the test, regardless of the outcome, such as going to a movie or getting ice cream.

When you are taking the test, if you find yourself beginning to feel anxious, remind yourself that you know the material. Visualize successfully completing the test. Then take a few deep, relaxing breaths and return to it. Work through the questions carefully but with confidence, knowing that you are capable of succeeding.

Developing a healthy mental approach to test taking will also aid in other areas of life. Test anxiety affects more than just the actual test—it can be damaging to your mental health and even contribute to depression. It's important to beat test anxiety before it becomes a problem for more than testing.

> **Review Video: Test Anxiety and Depression**
> Visit mometrix.com/academy and enter code: 904704

Study Strategy

Being prepared for the test is necessary to combat anxiety, but what does being prepared look like? You may study for hours on end and still not feel prepared. What you need is a strategy for test prep. The next few pages outline our recommended steps to help you plan out and conquer the challenge of preparation.

STEP 1: SCOPE OUT THE TEST

Learn everything you can about the format (multiple choice, essay, etc.) and what will be on the test. Gather any study materials, course outlines, or sample exams that may be available. Not only will this help you to prepare, but knowing what to expect can help to alleviate test anxiety.

STEP 2: MAP OUT THE MATERIAL

Look through the textbook or study guide and make note of how many chapters or sections it has. Then divide these over the time you have. For example, if a book has 15 chapters and you have five days to study, you need to cover three chapters each day. Even better, if you have the time, leave an extra day at the end for overall review after you have gone through the material in depth.

If time is limited, you may need to prioritize the material. Look through it and make note of which sections you think you already have a good grasp on, and which need review. While you are studying, skim quickly through the familiar sections and take more time on the challenging parts. Write out your plan so you don't get lost as you go. Having a written plan also helps you feel more in control of the study, so anxiety is less likely to arise from feeling overwhelmed at the amount to cover.

STEP 3: GATHER YOUR TOOLS

Decide what study method works best for you. Do you prefer to highlight in the book as you study and then go back over the highlighted portions? Or do you type out notes of the important information? Or is it helpful to make flashcards that you can carry with you? Assemble the pens, index cards, highlighters, post-it notes, and any other materials you may need so you won't be distracted by getting up to find things while you study.

If you're having a hard time retaining the information or organizing your notes, experiment with different methods. For example, try color-coding by subject with colored pens, highlighters, or post-it notes. If you learn better by hearing, try recording yourself reading your notes so you can listen while in the car, working out, or simply sitting at your desk. Ask a friend to quiz you from your flashcards, or try teaching someone the material to solidify it in your mind.

STEP 4: CREATE YOUR ENVIRONMENT

It's important to avoid distractions while you study. This includes both the obvious distractions like visitors and the subtle distractions like an uncomfortable chair (or a too-comfortable couch that makes you want to fall asleep). Set up the best study environment possible: good lighting and a comfortable work area. If background music helps you focus, you may want to turn it on, but otherwise keep the room quiet. If you are using a computer to take notes, be sure you don't have any other windows open, especially applications like social media, games, or anything else that could distract you. Silence your phone and turn off notifications. Be sure to keep water close by so you stay hydrated while you study (but avoid unhealthy drinks and snacks).

Also, take into account the best time of day to study. Are you freshest first thing in the morning? Try to set aside some time then to work through the material. Is your mind clearer in the afternoon or evening? Schedule your study session then. Another method is to study at the same time of day that you will take the test, so that your brain gets used to working on the material at that time and will be ready to focus at test time.

STEP 5: STUDY!

Once you have done all the study preparation, it's time to settle into the actual studying. Sit down, take a few moments to settle your mind so you can focus, and begin to follow your study plan. Don't give in to distractions or let yourself procrastinate. This is your time to prepare so you'll be ready to fearlessly approach the test. Make the most of the time and stay focused.

Of course, you don't want to burn out. If you study too long you may find that you're not retaining the information very well. Take regular study breaks. For example, taking five minutes out of every hour to walk briskly, breathing deeply and swinging your arms, can help your mind stay fresh.

As you get to the end of each chapter or section, it's a good idea to do a quick review. Remind yourself of what you learned and work on any difficult parts. When you feel that you've mastered the material, move on to the next part. At the end of your study session, briefly skim through your notes again.

But while review is helpful, cramming last minute is NOT. If at all possible, work ahead so that you won't need to fit all your study into the last day. Cramming overloads your brain with more information than it can process and retain, and your tired mind may struggle to recall even previously learned information when it is overwhelmed with last-minute study. Also, the urgent nature of cramming and the stress placed on your brain contribute to anxiety. You'll be more likely to go to the test feeling unprepared and having trouble thinking clearly.

So don't cram, and don't stay up late before the test, even just to review your notes at a leisurely pace. Your brain needs rest more than it needs to go over the information again. In fact, plan to finish your studies by noon or early afternoon the day before the test. Give your brain the rest of the day to relax or focus on other things, and get a good night's sleep. Then you will be fresh for the test and better able to recall what you've studied.

STEP 6: TAKE A PRACTICE TEST

Many courses offer sample tests, either online or in the study materials. This is an excellent resource to check whether you have mastered the material, as well as to prepare for the test format and environment.

Check the test format ahead of time: the number of questions, the type (multiple choice, free response, etc.), and the time limit. Then create a plan for working through them. For example, if you have 30 minutes to take a 60-question test, your limit is 30 seconds per question. Spend less time on the questions you know well so that you can take more time on the difficult ones.

If you have time to take several practice tests, take the first one open book, with no time limit. Work through the questions at your own pace and make sure you fully understand them. Gradually work up to taking a test under test conditions: sit at a desk with all study materials put away and set a timer. Pace yourself to make sure you finish the test with time to spare and go back to check your answers if you have time.

After each test, check your answers. On the questions you missed, be sure you understand why you missed them. Did you misread the question (tests can use tricky wording)? Did you forget the information? Or was it something you hadn't learned? Go back and study any shaky areas that the practice tests reveal.

Taking these tests not only helps with your grade, but also aids in combating test anxiety. If you're already used to the test conditions, you're less likely to worry about it, and working through tests until you're scoring well gives you a confidence boost. Go through the practice tests until you feel comfortable, and then you can go into the test knowing that you're ready for it.

Test Tips

On test day, you should be confident, knowing that you've prepared well and are ready to answer the questions. But aside from preparation, there are several test day strategies you can employ to maximize your performance.

First, as stated before, get a good night's sleep the night before the test (and for several nights before that, if possible). Go into the test with a fresh, alert mind rather than staying up late to study.

Try not to change too much about your normal routine on the day of the test. It's important to eat a nutritious breakfast, but if you normally don't eat breakfast at all, consider eating just a protein bar. If you're a coffee drinker, go ahead and have your normal coffee. Just make sure you time it so that the caffeine doesn't wear off right in the middle of your test. Avoid sugary beverages, and drink enough water to stay hydrated but not so much that you need a restroom break 10 minutes into the test. If your test isn't first thing in the morning, consider going for a walk or doing a light workout before the test to get your blood flowing.

Allow yourself enough time to get ready, and leave for the test with plenty of time to spare so you won't have the anxiety of scrambling to arrive in time. Another reason to be early is to select a good seat. It's helpful to sit away from doors and windows, which can be distracting. Find a good seat, get out your supplies, and settle your mind before the test begins.

When the test begins, start by going over the instructions carefully, even if you already know what to expect. Make sure you avoid any careless mistakes by following the directions.

Then begin working through the questions, pacing yourself as you've practiced. If you're not sure on an answer, don't spend too much time on it, and don't let it shake your confidence. Either skip it and come back later, or eliminate as many wrong answers as possible and guess among the remaining ones. Don't dwell on these questions as you continue—put them out of your mind and focus on what lies ahead.

Be sure to read all of the answer choices, even if you're sure the first one is the right answer. Sometimes you'll find a better one if you keep reading. But don't second-guess yourself if you do immediately know the answer. Your gut instinct is usually right. Don't let test anxiety rob you of the information you know.

If you have time at the end of the test (and if the test format allows), go back and review your answers. Be cautious about changing any, since your first instinct tends to be correct, but make sure you didn't misread any of the questions or accidentally mark the wrong answer choice. Look over any you skipped and make an educated guess.

At the end, leave the test feeling confident. You've done your best, so don't waste time worrying about your performance or wishing you could change anything. Instead, celebrate the successful

completion of this test. And finally, use this test to learn how to deal with anxiety even better next time.

Important Qualification

Not all anxiety is created equal. If your test anxiety is causing major issues in your life beyond the classroom or testing center, or if you are experiencing troubling physical symptoms related to your anxiety, it may be a sign of a serious physiological or psychological condition. If this sounds like your situation, we strongly encourage you to seek professional help.

How to Overcome Your Fear of Math

Not again. You're sitting in math class, look down at your test, and immediately start to panic. Your stomach is in knots, your heart is racing, and you break out in a cold sweat. You're staring at the paper, but everything looks like it's written in a foreign language. Even though you studied, you're blanking out on how to begin solving these problems.

Does this sound familiar? If so, then you're not alone! You may be like millions of other people who experience math anxiety. Anxiety about performing well in math is a common experience for students of all ages. In this article, we'll discuss what math anxiety is, common misconceptions about learning math, and tips and strategies for overcoming math anxiety.

What Is Math Anxiety?

Psychologist Mark H. Ashcraft explains math anxiety as a feeling of tension, apprehension, or fear that interferes with math performance. Having math anxiety negatively impacts people's beliefs about themselves and what they can achieve. It hinders achievement within the math classroom and affects the successful application of mathematics in the real world.

SYMPTOMS AND SIGNS OF MATH ANXIETY

To overcome math anxiety, you must recognize its symptoms. Becoming aware of the signs of math anxiety is the first step in addressing and resolving these fears.

NEGATIVE SELF-TALK

If you have math anxiety, you've most likely said at least one of these statements to yourself:

- "I hate math."
- "I'm not good at math."
- "I'm not a math person."

The way we speak to ourselves and think about ourselves matters. Our thoughts become our words, our words become our actions, and our actions become our habits. Thinking negatively about math creates a self-fulfilling prophecy. In other words, if you take an idea as a fact, then it will come true because your behaviors will align to match it.

AVOIDANCE

Some people who are fearful or anxious about math will tend to avoid it altogether. Avoidance can manifest in the following ways:

- Lack of engagement with math content
- Not completing homework and other assignments
- Not asking for help when needed
- Skipping class
- Avoiding math-related courses and activities

Avoidance is one of the most harmful impacts of math anxiety. If you steer clear of math at all costs, then you can't set yourself up for the success you deserve.

LACK OF MOTIVATION

Students with math anxiety may experience a lack of motivation. They may struggle to find the incentive to get engaged with what they view as a frightening subject. These students are often overwhelmed, making it difficult for them to complete or even start math assignments.

PROCRASTINATION

Another symptom of math anxiety is procrastination. Students may voluntarily delay or postpone their classwork and assignments, even if they know there will be a negative consequence for doing so. Additionally, they may choose to wait until the last minute to start projects and homework, even when they know they need more time to put forth their best effort.

PHYSIOLOGICAL REACTIONS

Many people with a fear of math experience physiological side effects. These may include an increase in heart rate, sweatiness, shakiness, nausea, and irregular breathing. These symptoms make it difficult to focus on the math content, causing the student even more stress and fear.

STRONG EMOTIONAL RESPONSES

Math anxiety also affects people on an emotional level. Responding to math content with strong emotions such as panic, anger, or despair can be a sign of math anxiety.

LOW TEST SCORES AND PERFORMANCE

Low achievement can be both a symptom and a cause of math anxiety. When someone does not take the steps needed to perform well on tests and assessments, they are less likely to pass. The more they perform poorly, the more they accept this poor performance as a fact that can't be changed.

FEELING ALONE

People who experience math anxiety feel like they are the only ones struggling, even if the math they are working on is challenging to many people. Feeling isolated in what they perceive as failure can trigger tension or nervousness.

FEELING OF PERMANENCY

Math anxiety can feel very permanent. You may assume that you are naturally bad at math and always will be. Viewing math as a natural ability rather than a skill that can be learned causes people to believe that nothing will help them improve. They take their current math abilities as fact and assume that they can't be changed. As a result, they give up, stop trying to improve, and avoid engaging with math altogether.

LACK OF CONFIDENCE

People with low self-confidence in math tend to feel awkward and incompetent when asked to solve a math problem. They don't feel comfortable taking chances or risks when problem-solving because they second-guess themselves and assume they are incorrect. They don't trust in their ability to learn the content and solve problems correctly.

PANIC

A general sense of unexplained panic is also a sign of math anxiety. You may feel a sudden sense of fear that triggers physical reactions, even when there is no apparent reason for such a response.

CAUSES OF MATH ANXIETY

Math anxiety can start at a young age and may have one or more underlying causes. Common causes of math anxiety include the following:

THE ATTITUDE OF PARENTS OR GUARDIANS

Parents often put pressure on their children to perform well in school. Although their intentions are usually good, this pressure can lead to anxiety, especially if the student is struggling with a subject or class.

Perhaps your parents or others in your life hold negative predispositions about math based on their own experiences. For instance, if your mother once claimed she was not good at math, then you might have incorrectly interpreted this as a predisposed trait that was passed down to you.

TEACHER INFLUENCE

Students often pick up on their teachers' attitudes about the content being taught. If a teacher is happy and excited about math, students are more likely to mirror these emotions. However, if a teacher lacks enthusiasm or genuine interest, then students are more inclined to disengage.

Teachers have a responsibility to cultivate a welcoming classroom culture that is accepting of mistakes. When teachers blame students for not understanding a concept, they create a hostile classroom environment where mistakes are not tolerated. This tension increases student stress and anxiety, creating conditions that are not conducive to inquiry and learning. Instead, when teachers normalize mistakes as a natural part of the problem-solving process, they give their students the freedom to explore and grapple with the math content. In such an environment, students feel comfortable taking chances because they are not afraid of being wrong.

Students need teachers that can help when they're having problems understanding difficult concepts. In doing so, educators may need to change how they teach the content. Since different people have unique learning styles, it's the job of the teacher to adapt to the needs of each student. Additionally, teachers should encourage students to explore alternate problem-solving strategies, even if it's not the preferred method of the educator.

FEAR OF BEING WRONG

Embarrassing situations can be traumatic, especially for young children and adolescents. These experiences can stay with people through their adult lives. Those with math anxiety may experience a fear of being wrong, especially in front of a group of peers. This fear can be paralyzing, interfering with the student's concentration and ability to focus on the problem at hand.

TIMED ASSESSMENTS

Timed assessments can help improve math fluency, but they often create unnecessary pressure for students to complete an unrealistic number of problems within a specified timeframe. Many studies have shown that timed assessments often result in increased levels of anxiety, reducing a student's overall competence and ability to problem-solve.

Debunking Math Myths

There are lots of myths about math that are related to the causes and development of math-related anxiety. Although these myths have been proven to be false, many people take them as fact. Let's go over a few of the most common myths about learning math.

MYTH: MEN ARE BETTER AT MATH THAN WOMEN

Math has a reputation for being a male-dominant subject, but this doesn't mean that men are inherently better at math than women. Many famous mathematical discoveries have been made by women. Katherine Johnson, Dame Mary Lucy Cartwright, and Marjorie Lee Brown are just a few of the many famous women mathematicians. Expecting to be good or bad at math because of your gender sets you up for stress and confusion. Math is a skill that can be learned, just like cooking or riding a bike.

MYTH: THERE IS ONLY ONE GOOD WAY TO SOLVE MATH PROBLEMS

There are many ways to get the correct answer when it comes to math. No two people have the same brain, so everyone takes a slightly different approach to problem-solving. Moreover, there isn't one way of problem-solving that's superior to another. Your way of working through a problem might differ from someone else's, and that is okay. Math can be a highly individualized process, so the best method for you should be the one that makes you feel the most comfortable and makes the most sense to you.

MYTH: MATH REQUIRES A GOOD MEMORY

For many years, mathematics was taught through memorization. However, learning in such a way hinders the development of critical thinking and conceptual understanding. These skill sets are much more valuable than basic memorization. For instance, you might be great at memorizing mathematical formulas, but if you don't understand what they mean, then you can't apply them to different scenarios in the real world. When a student is working from memory, they are limited in the strategies available to them to problem-solve. In other words, they assume there is only one correct way to do the math, which is the method they memorized. Having a variety of problem-solving options can help students figure out which method works best for them. Additionally, it provides students with a better understanding of how and why certain mathematical strategies work. While memorization can be helpful in some instances, it is not an absolute requirement for mathematicians.

MYTH: MATH IS NOT CREATIVE

Math requires imagination and intuition. Contrary to popular belief, it is a highly creative field. Mathematical creativity can help in developing new ways to think about and solve problems. Many people incorrectly assume that all things are either creative or analytical. However, this black-and-white view is limiting because the field of mathematics involves both creativity and logic.

MYTH: MATH ISN'T SUPPOSED TO BE FUN

Whoever told you that math isn't supposed to be fun is a liar. There are tons of math-based activities and games that foster friendly competition and engagement. Math is often best learned through play, and lots of mobile apps and computer games exemplify this.

Additionally, math can be an exceptionally collaborative and social experience. Studying or working through problems with a friend often makes the process a lot more fun. The excitement and satisfaction of solving a difficult problem with others is quite rewarding. Math can be fun if you look for ways to make it more collaborative and enjoyable.

MYTH: NOT EVERYONE IS CAPABLE OF LEARNING MATH

There's no such thing as a "math person." Although many people think that you're either good at math or you're not, this is simply not true. Everyone is capable of learning and applying mathematics. However, not everyone learns the same way. Since each person has a different learning style, the trick is to find the strategies and learning tools that work best for you. Some people learn best through hands-on experiences, and others find success through the use of visual aids. Others are auditory learners and learn best by hearing and listening. When people are overwhelmed or feel that math is too hard, it's often because they haven't found the learning strategy that works best for them.

MYTH: GOOD MATHEMATICIANS WORK QUICKLY AND NEVER MAKE MISTAKES

There is no prize for finishing first in math. It's not a race, and speed isn't a measure of your ability. Good mathematicians take their time to ensure their work is accurate. As you gain more experience and practice, you will naturally become faster and more confident.

Additionally, everyone makes mistakes, including good mathematicians. Mistakes are a normal part of the problem-solving process, and they're not a bad thing. The important thing is that we take the time to learn from our mistakes, understand where our misconceptions are, and move forward.

MYTH: YOU DON'T NEED MATH IN THE REAL WORLD

Our day-to-day lives are so infused with mathematical concepts that we often don't even realize when we're using math in the real world. In fact, most people tend to underestimate how much we do math in our everyday lives. It's involved in an enormous variety of daily activities such as shopping, baking, finances, and gardening, as well as in many careers, including architecture, nursing, design, and sales.

Tips and Strategies for Overcoming Math Anxiety

If your anxiety is getting in the way of your level of mathematical engagement, then there are lots of steps you can take. Check out the strategies below to start building confidence in math today.

FOCUS ON UNDERSTANDING, NOT MEMORIZATION

Don't drive yourself crazy trying to memorize every single formula or mathematical process. Instead, shift your attention to understanding concepts. Those who prioritize memorization over conceptual understanding tend to have lower achievement levels in math. Students who memorize may be able to complete some math, but they don't understand the process well enough to apply it to different situations. Memorization comes with time and practice, but it won't help alleviate math anxiety. On the other hand, conceptual understanding will give you the building blocks of knowledge you need to build up your confidence.

REPLACE NEGATIVE SELF-TALK WITH POSITIVE SELF-TALK

Start to notice how you think about yourself. Whenever you catch yourself thinking something negative, try replacing that thought with a positive affirmation. Instead of continuing the negative thought, pause to reframe the situation. For ideas on how to get started, take a look at the table below:

Instead of thinking...	Try thinking...
"I can't do this math." "I'm not a math person."	"I'm up for the challenge, and I'm training my brain in math."
"This problem is too hard."	"This problem is hard, so this might take some time and effort. I know I can do this."
"I give up."	"What strategies can help me solve this problem?"
"I made a mistake, so I'm not good at this."	"Everyone makes mistakes. Mistakes help me to grow and understand."
"I'll never be smart enough."	"I can figure this out, and I am smart enough."

PRACTICE MINDFULNESS

Practicing mindfulness and focusing on your breathing can help alleviate some of the physical symptoms of math anxiety. By taking deep breaths, you can remind your nervous system that you are not in immediate danger. Doing so will reduce your heart rate and help with any irregular breathing or shakiness. Taking the edge off of the physiological effects of anxiety will clear your mind, allowing your brain to focus its energy on problem-solving.

DO SOME MATH EVERY DAY

Think about learning math as if you were learning a foreign language. If you don't use it, you lose it. If you don't practice your math skills regularly, you'll have a harder time achieving comprehension and fluency. Set some amount of time aside each day, even if it's just for a few minutes, to practice. It might take some discipline to build a habit around this, but doing so will help increase your mathematical self-assurance.

USE ALL OF YOUR RESOURCES

Everyone has a different learning style, and there are plenty of resources out there to support all learners. When you get stuck on a math problem, think about the tools you have access to, and use them when applicable. Such resources may include flashcards, graphic organizers, study guides, interactive notebooks, and peer study groups. All of these are great tools to accommodate your individual learning style. Finding the tools and resources that work for your learning style will give you the confidence you need to succeed.

REALIZE THAT YOU AREN'T ALONE

Remind yourself that lots of other people struggle with math anxiety, including teachers, nurses, and even successful mathematicians. You aren't the only one who panics when faced with a new or challenging problem. It's probably much more common than you think. Realizing that you aren't alone in your experience can help put some distance between yourself and the emotions you feel about math. It also helps to normalize the anxiety and shift your perspective.

ASK QUESTIONS

If there's a concept you don't understand and you've tried everything you can, then it's okay to ask for help! You can always ask your teacher or professor for help. If you're not learning math in a traditional classroom, you may want to join a study group, work with a tutor, or talk to your friends. More often than not, you aren't the only one of your peers who needs clarity on a mathematical concept. Seeking understanding is a great way to increase self-confidence in math.

REMEMBER THAT THERE'S MORE THAN ONE WAY TO SOLVE A PROBLEM

Since everyone learns differently, it's best to focus on understanding a math problem with an approach that makes sense to you. If the way it's being taught is confusing to you, don't give up. Instead, work to understand the problem using a different technique. There's almost always more than one problem-solving method when it comes to math. Don't get stressed if one of them doesn't make sense to you. Instead, shift your focus to what does make sense. Chances are high that you know more than you think you do.

VISUALIZATION

Visualization is the process of creating images in your mind's eye. Picture yourself as a successful, confident mathematician. Think about how you would feel and how you would behave. What would your work area look like? How would you organize your belongings? The more you focus on something, the more likely you are to achieve it. Visualizing teaches your brain that you can achieve whatever it is that you want. Thinking about success in mathematics will lead to acting like a successful mathematician. This, in turn, leads to actual success.

FOCUS ON THE EASIEST PROBLEMS FIRST

To increase your confidence when working on a math test or assignment, try solving the easiest problems first. Doing so will remind you that you are successful in math and that you do have what it takes. This process will increase your belief in yourself, giving you the confidence you need to tackle more complex problems.

FIND A SUPPORT GROUP

A study buddy, tutor, or peer group can go a long way in decreasing math-related anxiety. Such support systems offer lots of benefits, including a safe place to ask questions, additional practice with mathematical concepts, and an understanding of other problem-solving explanations that may work better for you. Equipping yourself with a support group is one of the fastest ways to eliminate math anxiety.

REWARD YOURSELF FOR WORKING HARD

Recognize the amount of effort you're putting in to overcome your math anxiety. It's not an easy task, so you deserve acknowledgement. Surround yourself with people who will provide you with the positive reinforcement you deserve.

Remember, You Can Do This!

Conquering a fear of math can be challenging, but there are lots of strategies that can help you out. Your own beliefs about your mathematical capabilities can limit your potential. Working toward a growth mindset can have a tremendous impact on decreasing math-related anxiety and building confidence. By knowing the symptoms of math anxiety and recognizing common misconceptions about learning math, you can develop a plan to address your fear of math. Utilizing the strategies discussed can help you overcome this anxiety and build the confidence you need to succeed.

Thank You

We at Mometrix would like to extend our heartfelt thanks to you, our friend and patron, for allowing us to play a part in your journey. It is a privilege to serve people from all walks of life who are unified in their commitment to building the best future they can for themselves.

The preparation you devote to these important testing milestones may be the most valuable educational opportunity you have for making a real difference in your life. We encourage you to put your heart into it—that feeling of succeeding, overcoming, and yes, conquering will be well worth the hours you've invested.

We want to hear your story, your struggles and your successes, and if you see any opportunities for us to improve our materials so we can help others even more effectively in the future, please share that with us as well. **The team at Mometrix would be absolutely thrilled to hear from you!** So please, send us an email (support@mometrix.com) and let's stay in touch.

> **If you'd like some additional help, check out these other resources we offer for your exam:**
> **http://MometrixFlashcards.com/Iowa**

Additional Bonus Material

Due to our efforts to try to keep this book to a manageable length, we've created a link that will give you access to all of your additional bonus material:

mometrix.com/bonus948/iowal12g6